RICHARD PRICE
Philosopher

From an engraving by Holloway in the National Museum of Wales
after an original painting by Sir Benjamin West
now in the possession of the Royal Society

RICHARD PRICE

PHILOSOPHER AND APOSTLE OF LIBERTY

By ROLAND THOMAS, M.A.

Director of the Welsh Holiday School

OXFORD UNIVERSITY PRESS

LONDON: HUMPHREY MILFORD

1924

PRINTED IN ENGLAND
AT THE OXFORD UNIVERSITY PRESS
BY FREDERICK HALL

PREFACE

THIS volume is intended to be a brief presentation of Richard Price's life and work. Apart from the inadequate, and, unfortunately, often inaccurate, *Memoirs* of him by his nephew William Morgan, published over a hundred years ago, there does not exist at the present moment a single book devoted to him. This volume is intended to help fill this gap and so contribute a little towards rescuing Price from an oblivion utterly undeserved. Its bias is definitely biographical, but a sufficient account is given of Price's chief works to show their importance, and, it is hoped, to establish for him claims which have not hitherto been sufficiently known and emphasized. Price was a truly great man, a seer and a prophet, and a dominant figure in epoch-making periods, many of his ideas formulating the age he lived in, and some anticipating the future by nearly two centuries. For he was a profound thinker who attained the highest eminence, and merited lasting fame, in several fields of human knowledge. He deserves a far more exhaustive work than the present volume claims to be ; but should this little contribution in the smallest measure prepare the way for such a work, it will have amply fulfilled its pretensions.

Thanks are gratefully tendered to various institutions mentioned in the foot-notes as authorities for information ;

to those libraries named in the Bibliography for lists for collation ; to the Massachusetts Historical Society for the gift of a copy of the Price letters ; to Dr. Williams's Library for valuable loans and unfailing courtesy ; and to Mr. Stephen K. Jones, Sub-Librarian of Dr. Williams's Library, for the loan of an extremely rare copy, which is his private possession, of Price's manuscript, and for his kind permission to reproduce it.

R. T.

BRECON,
   Jan. 5, 1924.

CONTENTS

CHAPTER I

CHAPTER II

CHAPTER III

CHAPTER IV

CHAPTER V

CHAPTER VI

CHAPTER VII

CHAPTER VIII

CHAPTER IX

CHAPTER X

ILLUSTRATIONS

CHAPTER I

THE eighteenth century, within which the life of Richard
Price falls, was a period wherein influences originating in
the seventeenth century played a dominant part. The
main feature of eighteenth-century thought in general
was Rationalism. It arose partly as a reaction against
the element of mysticism which had been prominent in
the preceding century, and partly as a natural consequence
of the conquests which reason had made in the fields of
physical science at the hands of Bacon, Galileo, Gassendi,
Copernicus, Kepler, and Newton. It underlay the thought
of the century in almost every field. Nowhere was the
tendency to make reason the final authority more manifest
than in politics and religion.

Politically, the outstanding event of the preceding
century, as, also, it is one of the outstanding events of
world history, was the Revolution of 1688. It destroyed
for ever the theory of the divine right of kings, and established the right, which might in a more proper sense be
called the right divine, of the people. The political history
of the eighteenth century consists of the effort to make
actual what that event had made possible. Though
writing before the former century had closed, John Locke,

B

seeking to justify the Revolution and its principles, and basing his argument upon a vigorously logical appeal to reason, became the typical representative of the new attitude in the field of politics and government.

In religion, the rationalist spirit found expression in Deism, with its rejection of prophecy, miracle, and revelation. Deism, however, was short-lived, and had almost completely died out by the middle of the eighteenth century. Vigorously opposed to it, though, like it, deriving its impetus from the same underlying element of thought, was Arianism, a denial of the Trinity slightly less remote from orthodoxy than Socinianism.

The seventeenth century saw the rise of Nonconformity or Dissent, whose connexion with the beliefs just mentioned came to be as marked as that of the Established Church. Under the name of Puritanism, Dissent had really existed and even become a national force before that century. In spite of stern and determined legislation directed against it, Nonconformity strengthened and grew, but, though it had been granted toleration and indulgence in the course of about fifty years following 1662, it was, nevertheless, still on its defensive throughout the eighteenth century. In its strenuous activity, it produced, during much of that time, great work of permanent value.

It is through the rise of Nonconformity that the life of Richard Price is best approached. The effect of the Act of Uniformity, the immediate cause of Dissent, was as far-reaching in Wales as in England. The most notable of the ejected clergy was the Rev. Samuel Jones, Vicar of Llangynwyd, in the County of Glamorgan. He was a friend of Baxter, and as great a scholar as he was a preacher. He had been in the parish five years, having been ' approved ' by Cromwell's Triers on his removal there from Taunton in 1657.[1] Upon his ejection he removed to Brynllywarch, a farmhouse belonging to Rees Powell, his father-in-law, who was a wealthy gentleman. In spite of frequent imprisonment Samuel Jones dedicated his life to his work. He continued it in his own home and in neighbouring farmhouses, including Tymaen, and, later, Cildeudy, the property of his father-in-law. Brynllywarch and Cildeudy became, before 1669, the regular meeting-places of the little congregation, both remaining so for about thirty years, that is, until the death of Samuel Jones in 1697, and Cildeudy, at least, for about another twenty years. Then, somewhere between 1715 and 1720, two ' Meeting Houses ' were built, one in the neighbouring town of Bridgend, and the other at Bettws, not far from Brynllywarch. Like many another of the ejected clergymen, Samuel Jones, who had been a Fellow and Tutor of Jesus College, Oxford, combined teaching with preaching. Soon after his ejection he opened a school at Brynllywarch, conducting it with marked success until his death. Two famous contemporaries of his in Wales were Stephen Hughes and Vavasor Powell, who, like him, first belonged to the Anglican Church, but, unlike him, gave themselves to itinerant preaching and the founding of churches, the one in the Congregational and the other in the Baptist cause. Howel Harris, doing the same work for Methodism, came half a century later. Samuel Jones's school or ' Academy '—the title by which all dissenting schools of the same character became known—is the forerunner of all the Welsh Colleges in that it marks the very beginning of education of university standard in Wales, while the

[1] Thomas Richards, *Religious Developments in Wales (1654–1662)*, pp. 11, 22.

Theological Colleges now at Brecon and Carmarthen are
descended from it directly, though by divergent lines.
Moreover, the College at Carmarthen was the first institution in Wales from which students graduated in Arts.[1]
Its curriculum was not that of the Grammar Schools of
the day, but followed, and even went beyond, that of
the older universities. When it is remembered that these
latter, the only universities then existing in England,
were closed to all save members of the Established Church,
it is seen how substantial were the advantages which the
Brynllywarch ' Academy ' offered. The best families,
both of Anglican and of Nonconformist persuasion, sent
their sons to it, and most of the ministers of Wales, for
a period of thirty-eight years closing with 1797, received
their education there. Among them was James Owen,
who became a noted tutor as head of a similar Academy
in Shrewsbury. It was self-supporting for many years,
but eventually both the Presbyterian Fund Board, which
had been established in 1689, and the Congregational
Fund Board, which had been established in 1695, gave
it financial support.

Three families who were parishioners of Samuel Jones
before his ejection deserve mention : the Mansels of
Margam, the Thomases of Cefn Ydfa, and the Prices of
Tynton. The last two left the Established Church with
their ejected clergyman in 1662, and became members
of his Dissenting congregation. The sons of the three
families attended the Academy. The Cefn Ydfa and the
Tynton families became connected by marriage.

The head of the Tynton family in the last quarter of
the seventeenth century was Rees Price. Both he and his

[1] Jeremy, *The Presbyterian Fund and Dr. Daniel Williams's
Trust*, p. 238.

wife, Catherine, lived to a great age—Rees to 91 years, and his wife to 90. They were deeply religious people.[1] Their elder son, born in 1673, was named, after his father, Rees ; and their younger son, Samuel ; while their only daughter was named, after her mother, Catherine. She married, in 1703, William Thomas, the son of Cefn Ydfa, and went to live there. William and Catherine Thomas, whose married life, owing to the death of the former in 1707, lasted less than four years, had two children : a son, William, the younger of the two, who died in infancy a few days after his father; and a daughter, Ann, who lived to become the renowned Ann Thomas, ' The Maid of Cefn Ydfa ', whose tragically romantic life is a household story in Wales. Both Rees and Samuel, the sons of Tynton, became Nonconformist ministers of religion. Samuel proceeded to the Academy conducted by Timothy Jollie at Attercliffe, near Sheffield, to complete his training. Thomas Secker, who afterwards became Archbishop of Canterbury, received part of his training at the same Academy, he being an instance of many eminent clergymen of the Established Church who were educated at a Dissenting Academy, and whose residence in the University was mainly, if not solely, for the purpose of fulfilling the necessary conditions for admission to Holy Orders. From his studies at Attercliffe Samuel Price was

[1] Rees's tombstone in the Chancel of the Bettws Church bears this verse :

> A faithful, pious, painful man,
>   And zealous to the end,
> For to promote the cause of Christ
>   And on him to attend ;
> Lyes here asleep, advising all
>   To live to Christ their Lord,
> To work in haste, while He to them
>   Doth life and time afford.

called, in 1703, the year of his sister's marriage to the son of Cefn Ydfa, to assist the celebrated hymn-writer Isaac Watts in the pastorate of a congregation of Independents, or Congregationalists, worshipping in St. Mary Axe, Bury Street, London. Ten years later, at Watts's expressed desire, he was ordained to the office of joint pastor, and henceforth he bore the whole pastoral responsibility, Watts being an invalid. He remained Watts's colleague until the latter's death in 1748, having then laboured with him for the long period of forty-five years. He further continued as pastor until he died eight years later.

Meanwhile, Rees, the elder son, had been called, about 1695, to assist his pastor and tutor, Samuel Jones, in the pastoral care of the congregations worshipping in Brynllywarch and Cildeudy. Upon the death of Samuel Jones, two years later, Rees Price succeeded him both as pastor and as tutor of the Academy. Rees Price's theological views were those of extreme Calvinism, and owing to these, no doubt, the Presbyterian Fund Board withdrew its support from the Academy, and gave it to an Academy which was opened by Roger Griffith at Abergavenny. Rees Price, however, still got support from the Congregational Fund Board. Roger Griffith soon joined the Church of England, becoming, in 1702, Archdeacon of Brecon, and his Academy, which is correctly regarded as a continuation collateral with Rees Price's, of the Brynllywarch Academy, lapsed. Among those who were educated under Griffith was Samuel Jones who became famous as the tutor of Tewkesbury Academy. The Academy under Rees Price can be traced up to 1704, this being the last date of any record of him in the minutes of the Congregational Fund Board, but he continued it without support for many years more, after four of which another Academy arose to perpetuate Brynllywarch. In 1708 both Fund Boards again joined in supporting this Academy set up in that year at Carmarthen by William Evans, who had studied at the Academy conducted by the famous Rees Prydderch at Ystrad Walter, near Llandovery.[1]

Rees Price, having inherited his father's estate, lived at Tynton, and pursued his pastoral work. He was a strong man, of intellect as of will, and led a many-sided life. Like his pastor and tutor, Samuel Jones, who attained to the presidency thereof, he belonged to the recognized bardic fraternity of Glamorgan, or ' Gorsedd Tir Iarll '. He was twice married. His first wife, a Miss Gibbon, is said to have been ' not only rich but saving to the verge of eccentricity '. Of this marriage there were four children : an eldest son whose name is uncertain,[2] John, Samuel, and Mary. All of them were grown up when Rees Price was left a widower. His second wife was Catherine, the youngest daughter of Dr. Richards, Oldcastle, Bridgend, who had a good practice in that town and was highly respected there. Catherine Richards was young—twenty years younger than Rees Price—very beautiful, and a most delightful woman. Of this marriage there were three children, one son and two daughters : Richard, Sarah, and Elizabeth. Richard, the eldest child of the second marriage, and the youngest son of the family, is our subject. It is interesting to note that he was the cousin of the Maid of Cefn Ydfa, his father and her mother being, as we have seen, brother and sister. It was his father, Rees Price, who officiated at the baptism of the young Maid at Cefn Ydfa ' amid great pomp and family

---

[1] This history may be followed in greater detail in Jeremy, *The Presbyterian Fund* ; Rees and Thomas, *Hanes Eglwysi Annibynol Cymru* (two vols.) ; and Bogue and Bennett, *History of Dissenters,* (four vols.).

[2] See p. 14, *infra*.

rejoicing ' in 1704. At the death of his brother-in-law, the Maid's father, a few years later, Rees Price was appointed guardian of the Cefn Ydfa children, one of whom, we have seen, died within a few days. Rees Price, therefore, must have spent much of his time at Cefn Ydfa with his widowed sister and her only daughter Ann. At least, all the clerical part of the management of affairs there must have devolved upon him, for his sister, though coming from as enlightened a home as any of those days, could not even sign her name.[1] In fact, everything points to his having had a considerable share in the stern shaping of the course of Ann Thomas's life with a view to frustrating the love she and Will Hopkin, a working man with bardic pretensions living in the neighbourhood, bore for each other, and to betrothing her to Anthony Maddocks, the son of the well-to-do lawyer of that name who was legal adviser to both the Cefn Ydfa and the Tynton families.[2]

Richard Price was born at Tynton on February 23, 1723. He was thus only four years old when on June 16, 1727, the sad Maid, his cousin, died of a broken heart, and he could not have more than barely remembered her. Tynton is situated in the parish of Llangeinor, on the hill-side on the left bank of the River Garw, a tributary of the River Ogwr, a Glamorganshire stream emptying into the Bristol Channel. A few miles lower down, on the Ogwr, and on the western edge of the fertile Vale of Glamorgan, stands Bridgend, then one of the most important towns in Wales and the centre of the life and activities not only of the country immediately

[1] See her signature with a × to the marriage settlement of her daughter, given in full in T. C. Evans (Cadrawd), *History of Llangynwyd Parish*, pp. 96–102.

[2] Ibid., pp. 92–6.

Photograph by Carver, Bridgend.

TYNTON, LLANGEINOR, GLAMORGANSHIRE

The Birthplace of Richard Price

surrounding it but also of much of the county of Glamorgan. The Prices owned substantial property in the district apart from Tynton. It is certain that they endowed the cause for which the two chapels at Bettws and Bridgend were built—a cause to which Samuel Price of London, Rees's brother, also gave a small sum—but whether it was by setting aside a farm, or by giving a sum of £200 and three houses in Newcastle, Bridgend, is not certain. They were, therefore, in comfortable circumstances and had high social standing, but they were by no means engrossed in the affairs of this world. The atmosphere of the house when Richard's father was its head was, as it had been also in his grandfather's day and for many a generation, distinctly religious. After the father's second marriage the presence of a sweet and charming personality in the person of Richard's mother brought just that gentle influence which, owing to the extreme austerity of the Prices, the home had lacked. Rees Price's rule was in a particular sense that of law. Catherine Price's rule was especially that of love, and she drew from her young son in return generous love for her. Richard inherited his father's strength without his austerity ; while that love of all sentient beings, and particularly of all mankind, which played such a controlling part in her son's later life, must have received powerful stimulus from his mother.

It was his father's wish that Richard should enter business, and it may be that had the father lived long enough he would have realized that wish, though the studious, reflective temperament of the boy would have proved a difficulty in his way. It is well for mankind that, for whatever reason, the father's wish was not realized. The boy's education was begun early. He learnt his rudiments partly from a family governess and partly from a Mr. Peters living in the vicinity, who became a minister later, and for whom he had a high regard. At an early age, certainly before he was ten, and possibly before he was eight, he was placed in a school in Bridgend, but he was taken from there after a short stay owing, it is said, to his master's bad temper. He was sent to a school conducted by Joseph Simmons, a dissenting minister and first pastor of the Church now known as Maesyrhaf, at Neath, where also some years before there had studied Lewis Rees, afterwards of Llanbrynmair and Mynyddbach, a descendant of John Penry [1] and father of Dr. Abraham Rees. It was to the Academy conducted by Richard's father that Lewis Rees went from Neath.[2] After about two years there, Richard went, in 1735, to a school conducted most successfully from 1730 to 1750 by Samuel Jones, a dissenting minister, at Pentwyn, in the parish of Llanon, Carmarthenshire. It deserves notice that there were three Samuel Joneses who were famous schoolmasters in that period, though they were not exactly contemporaries. They were : Samuel Jones, of Brynllywarch, whom we have already noticed; Samuel Jones, of Pentwyn, or Capel Seion, whom we are now noticing; and Samuel Jones, of Tewkesbury, whom we have merely mentioned already and shall notice presently. Samuel Jones, of Pentwyn, was a truly worthy man whose religious principles his young pupil greatly admired ' for their candour and liberality '. He had imbibed Arian opinions, and his pupil seems to have been impressed by them. Rees Price found his son during one of his vacations at Tynton reading a volume of sermons by Dr. Samuel Clarke, a well-known Arian and a still better known philosopher. The

---

[1] Article on Penry by Dr. Abraham Rees in his *New Cyclopedia*.
[2] Peter, *Hanes Crefydd yn Nghymru*, p. 665.

father was so angry at his son's conduct that he seized the book in a rage and threw it into the fire. The three years which Richard spent at Pentwyn form a distinct and most influential factor in his mental and religious development thereafter. Owen Rees, who became minister of Hen Dy Cwrdd, the noted Unitarian chapel, Aberdare, and grandfather of Thomas Rees, the historian of Welsh Nonconformity, a well-known Unitarian, and secretary to the Presbyterian Fund Board, also studied under Samuel Jones. From Pentwyn Richard proceeded, in 1738, to the Rev. Vavasor Griffiths's Academy, at Talgarth, in Breconshire. This was a continuation of the Brynllywarch Academy, having moved, as was its wont, whithersoever a capable tutor was found. It had been successively, as we have seen, under the charge of Samuel Jones, Roger Griffith, and Rees Price, and, after the lapse of four years, under that of William Evans, who conducted it at Carmarthen from 1708 to 1718, and Thomas Perrott, who continued it in the same town from 1718 to 1733. In the latter year it was removed to another district, where a tutor was available in the person of Vavasor Griffiths, and where it remained until the death of the tutor in 1741.[1]

It was really held, it appears, in three different places, with Vavasor Griffiths acting in a tutorial capacity at each of the three : Maesgwyn, near Presteign, in Radnorshire ; Llwynllwyd, near Hay, in Breconshire ; and Chancefield, in the town of Talgarth, in Breconshire.[2] Both the immortal William Williams, of Pantycelyn,

[1] This noted divine and schoolmaster was buried in Bugeildy, Radnorshire.

[2] For a full discussion of the questions of the location of the Academy and the tutorship thereat see the 'Note on the Welsh Dissenting Academy ' at the end of the volume, pp. 164–70.

' the Sweet Singer of Wales ', and the world's greatest hymn-writer, and, a few years earlier, Howell Harris, the great revivalist and founder of Methodism in Wales, were educated at Llwynllwyd. Richard Price, however, was educated at Chancefield.[1] He entered, probably, in 1738, and remained until 1740. It is important to notice, not only that Howell Harris—who did for the revival in Wales much the same service that Wesley did for it in England, and who, like Wesley, left a wealth of records in diaries and letters—was then carrying his message throughout the length and breadth of Wales, but also that he was on terms of close friendship with Vavasor Griffiths, the tutor at Chancefield, and that he used to visit the Academy and the young Academicians there,[2] Chancefield being only two miles distant from Trevecca, Harris's home. Richard Price, therefore, must have heard Harris a number of times, and must have, like the great Williams, of Pantycelyn, a year or so before, come under the influence of the thunder of his eloquence. Harris's Calvinism in theology, however, does not seem to have been sufficient to turn the pronounced anti-Calvin tendency which had already shown itself in young Price's incipient theological system.

Vavasor Griffiths, Price's tutor, had studied at the Tewkesbury Academy under Samuel Jones, where such famous men as Archbishop Thomas Secker, who had already attended Attercliffe Academy, Bishop Butler, Dr. Chandler, and Andrew Gifford, the founder of the ' Gifford Lectures ' had also studied. Samuel Jones was a Cardiganshire man, who, after attending the Academies at Abergavenny, under Roger Griffith, at Knells, Radnor-

[1] For the facts on which this view is based see the ' Note on the Welsh Dissenting Academy ' at the end of the volume.
[2] Ibid.

shire, under John Weaver,[1] and at Shrewsbury, under
James Owen, had proceeded to the Continent and studied
under the learned Perizonius, at Leyden.[2] One is not
surprised, therefore, that his Academy, established at
Gloucester about 1708, and removed to Tewkesbury about
1712, where it remained until his death about 1720, was
' a most flourishing one ', and ' famed for as much learning as any one seminary among the Nonconformists '.
Secker called it an ' extraordinary place of education '.
Mathematics and Theology, including Moral Philosophy,
received considerable attention there. This suggests the
likelihood of Vavasor Griffiths's having established the
same tradition at Maesgwyn, Llwynllwyd, and Chancefield, and that Richard Price, therefore, came under its
influence. In any case, Vavasor Griffiths was a man of
excellent education and training. Bogue and Bennett
say that the Tewkesbury institution was transferred to
Carmarthen and amalgamated with the Academy there,
and that the ' public library ' belonging to the former
was removed to Carmarthen ' with the benevolent design
of educating ministers for the Churches in Wales ' ; [3]
but it is also said that the only foundation for the former
statement is the fact ' that the Library was sent there '.[4]
David Peter, however, also definitely asserts the amal-
gamation,[5] whereas Jeremy says that there is no evidence
of even the Library having been removed there.[6] Vavasor
Griffiths received the support of both the Presbyterian

---

[1] See Peter, *Hanes Crefydd yn Nghymru*, pp. 569–70, and Parker,
Dissenting Academies in England, passim. Knill, Knell, or Knells
is to-day a Hereford parish adjoining the Radnorshire parish of Old
Radnor.   [2] Parker, ibid.

[3] Bogue and Bennett, *History of Dissenters*, vol. iii, p. 293.

[4] Parker, ibid., p. 101.

[5] Peter, ibid., pp. 570 n., 682.

[6] Jeremy, *The Presbyterian Fund and Dr. Williams's Trust*, p. 40.

and the Congregational Fund Boards in his tutorial
work. On his death the Academy was removed to
Haverfordwest, and thence soon back to Carmarthen.
During the tutorship of Samuel Thomas, 1751–66, at
the latter place, and owing to his Arian opinions, the Congregational Fund Board withheld its further support, and,
in 1755, set up another Academy at Abergavenny, under
David Jardine—just as the Presbyterian Fund Board
formerly set up another, also at Abergavenny, when,
owing to his extreme Calvinism, it refused to support
Rees Price. The Academy at Carmarthen went on
successfully, and, except for some eleven years which it
spent at Swansea, has been located there ever since.
It is now known as the Presbyterian College. The
Academy set up at Abergavenny also prospered, and,
after moving successively to Oswestry, Wrexham,
Llanfyllin, and Newtown, found its way to Brecon,
where it is located at present. It is now known as the
Congregational, or, to commemorate its origin, the
' Memorial ' College. Abergavenny, it may be noted,
was the home of yet a third Academy, one established
by the Baptists, under Micah Thomas, in 1807.

Richard Price was completing his first year at Chancefield when his father died suddenly, at Tynton, on June 28,
1739. Rees Price had always expressed his intention
of leaving the property he had acquired by his first
marriage to the children of that marriage. But he left
those children not only that portion, but also the greater
portion of his own fortune. He made his son John his heir,
passing over his eldest son who was then ' practising physik '
at Newport, and who survived his disappointment but
a short time.[1] John had married an heiress, Catherine
Williams, who, by her relationship with the Powells, was

[1] See p. 7, *supra*.

connected with Llangynwyd, and through whom he came into possession of Park, a property at the eastern end of the County. Rees Price's second wife, now a widow, and her children were left comparatively poor. Richard's portion was £400, and, characteristically, he gave the sum to his widowed mother and sisters. They now left Tynton, going to live in a small house in Bridgend. Richard was able to continue his education at Chancefield, where he was educated and boarded for five pounds a year. The deepest attachment existed between him and his mother and sisters. More than once he walked the whole distance between Talgarth and Bridgend, crossing the mountains, to visit them. On one occasion, during the exceptionally hard winter of 1739–40, he made the journey when the ground was everywhere thickly covered with snow. It was to see his mother who was then lying very ill. In a few months, on June 4, 1740, less than a year after the death of her husband, and at the early age of forty-seven, she died. Richard was present with his two sisters at their mother's death. The patience and sweetness with which she had borne for twelve months the hardship imposed upon her made a deep impression upon him, and he used often to speak of the tranquillity and joy with which she viewed the approaches of death and the prospect of a better world. His grief at her loss confirmed him in his serious turn of mind, and made him now decide, as he had been for some time strongly inclined, to enter the Dissenting ministry.

Deprived of both his parents, Richard turned for help and advice to his uncle, Samuel Price, the co-pastor of Isaac Watts. Having no means of going to London, he sought the assistance of his brother John, the heir of his father's fortune. John, in obliging his striving young brother, addressed him : ' Dick, your situation gives you some claim to my assistance ; my horse is at your service for the first twenty miles of your journey.' This very generous brother took care to send a servant along to bring the horse back from Cardiff. Richard, with his bundle in his hand, continued the journey as far as Bristol on foot, availing himself as he could of the assistance of passing carriages. Setting off thence in a broad-wheeled waggon he at length covered the remainder of his wearisome journey. It was his uncle's wish, as it was his own, that he should continue his education. He was accordingly entered at the Dissenting Academy which had been founded by a Mr. Coward of Walthamstow. This wealthy gentleman had also instituted ' lectures ' at Lime Street, Bury Street, and Little St. Helens. At each of these places the lecture course had as its purpose the defence of Calvinism. Samuel Price, Richard's uncle, was one of the six ministers who delivered the Bury Street course.[1] Coward, in leaving his great fortune ' to pious purposes ' intended that it should be ' limited to the support of the Calvinistic doctrine'. But the professional gentlemen who drew up the will ' expressed it in such terms as to leave the trustees at full liberty to apply it to the support of whatever they might judge to be the cause of Christ among Protestant Dissenters '. For many years this fund supported ' two very respectable and flourishing institutions for the education of dissenting ministers ', one ' in the vicinity of London ', this being that which Price entered, and the other ' in the country ', first at Northampton, and afterwards at Daventry. It was during this period that the Coward trust was at the height of its usefulness. To the trustees ' the whole dissenting interest looked up as its patrons and benefactors ; and

Wilson, *Dissenting Churches*, vol. ii, pp. 212, 244, 253, 263.

from one or other of their institutions most of the respectable congregations were supplied with well-educated
ministers '.[1] The Academy was often known, after its
founder, as ' Coward's Academy '. It was supported by the
Congregational Fund Board. Richard Price was a student
in it from 1740 to 1744. At that time it was located in
Tenter-alley, Moorfields. Its principal tutor was John
Eames, F.R.S., who was assisted by Joseph Densham.
John Eames became principal tutor in 1734, on the death
of Dr. Thomas Ridgley, whom he had assisted, and he
filled the post with great distinction until his death on
June 29, 1744. He had been trained for the ministry,
but owing to an impediment in his speech he preached
only one sermon in his life. He was acknowledged to be
a great scholar. Isaac Watts once described him as
' the most learned man I ever knew '. His knowledge of
classical literature was very extensive, but he was best
known for his profound knowledge of mathematics and
science, and his learning in these subjects procured for him
the acquaintance and friendship of Sir Isaac Newton, to
whom, on occasions, he proved himself very useful. It
was Newton who introduced him to the Royal Society,
of which he became a Fellow, and by which he was
employed, in conjunction with another, to prepare and
publish an abridgement of the Transactions. Among
pupils of his who became famous are Dr. Samuel Morton
Savage, John Howard, the prison reformer, Thomas
Secker, Archbishop of Canterbury, whom we have already
noticed at two other Academies, and Richard Price. He was
succeeded in the principal tutorship by Dr. David Jennings.
Joseph Densham had been a pupil under Eames before

---

[1] Belsham, *Memoirs of the late Reverend Theophilus Lindsey*,
pp. 218–19 *n.*

he became his assistant. He, too, had a reputation for mathematical and classical learning, and was, besides, a theologian of note. He was a greatly-loved man. John Howard, before going on one of his journeys, gave him an unlimited order to draw upon his banker for whatever money he might want. He is credited with having had a hand in the compilation of Howard's first book on prisons. On the death of Eames he retired from his tutorial office, in spite of the earnest efforts of Jennings, the succeeding tutor, to retain his services. After preaching occasionally for a short time, he relinquished the ministry and followed various secular employments. Upon Densham's retirement from it, the assistant tutorship was filled by Dr. Samuel Morton Savage, who was chosen also first to assist and then to succeed Samuel Price in Watts's pastorate.

On the death of Eames and the appointment of Jennings as principal tutor in 1744, the institution was removed from Tenter-alley, Moorfields, to Well-close-square, the lectures being delivered in Dr. Savage's house. On the death of Jennings in 1762, another removal was made to Hoxton, Dr. Savage becoming principal tutor and Dr. Andrew Kippis and Dr. Abraham Rees, son of Rev. Lewis Rees of Llanbrynmair and Mynyddbach, assistant tutors, the latter of the two, Dr. Rees, also succeeding Dr. Savage. A notable student of the Academy in its Hoxton period and during the principal tutorship of Rees was William Godwin, who became ' the apostle of Universal Benevolence ' and a celebrated Revolutionary.[1] After quite an illustrious career, the Academy ceased to exist independently in 1785,[2]

[1] Kegan Paul, *William Godwin ; His Friends and Contemporaries*, vol. i. pp. 14–15.

[2] Wilson, *Dissenting Churches*, vol. ii, pp. 73–4, and Bogue and Bennett. *History of Dissenters*, vol. iv, pp. 262–4.

and was merged in another. The cause, apparently, was the resignation in that year of the tutors, all of whom had become anti-Trinitarian, whereupon Coward's trustees ' feeling the support of two institutions a burden too oppressive, determined upon uniting them together at Daventry ',[1] under the direction of Thomas Belsham who was already, since 1781, theological tutor there, and who as yet had not relinquished Trinitarianism. After removing back to Northampton and thence to Wymondely and Byng Place, this institution was, in 1850, merged in New College, London.[2]

When his uncle entered Richard Price at the Academy he lodged him in Pudding Lane. The young man had not resided there a year when his health broke down and he was obliged to return to his sisters in Bridgend. His native air soon made him well again, and in the autumn he returned to London. He applied himself diligently to his studies, which were mainly devoted to mathematics, philosophy, and theology. He continued to arrive at theological conclusions which were not more pleasing to his uncle than they had been to his father. He made marked progress in all his work, and a gentleman who had become interested in him made him a present of ten pounds. Richard sent the whole of the money to his sisters. With his departure from the Academy after a very successful course in 1744, his formal education ends. He had always made the very best use of the excellent facilities offered him. The quality of the higher education he had received can be appreciated only when the significance of the Academy movement is understood. It is worth our while, therefore, taking a glance at what

[1] Belsham, *Memoirs of Lindsey*, pp. 218–19 n.
[2] Parker, *Dissenting Academies in England*, p. 141.

the Dissenting Academies did for education in the eighteenth century.[1]

Abbey, one of the historians of the English Church, says that ' Although the Church of England in Queen Anne's reign was, on the whole, by no means inactive in the cause of education, greater proportionate efforts were being made by Dissenters. . . . Some of their ablest men devoted themselves especially to the work of tuition, and established seminaries of such high repute that Churchmen of position and influence were sometimes tempted to send their sons to be educated there.'[2] The whole existence of the Academies covered less than a century and a half, 1662–1800. Coming into being with Dissent in 1662, it is to Dissent they entirely belonged, though they were attended by students who were members of the Episcopal Church. The Dissenting Academies are to be distinguished from the Dissenting Schools. The latter were ' charity foundations ' and ' differed probably little from the ordinary schools of the day '. The Dissenting Academies, on the other hand, were ' schools of university standing, and students went to them at the ordinary university age '. The course ' usually extended for four years ', and presupposed a general knowledge of classics. They were neither large nor very numerous— some of them even dying with their founders—but they became very important. Generally speaking, they fall into three periods with corresponding broad distinctions in their character : ' (1) those of the first period, 1663 to about 1690, founded by ejected ministers, in which, as

---

[1] The story is briefly but well told in Parker, *Dissenting Academies in England*, upon which the account here given, except where otherwise stated, is based.

[2] Abbey, *The English Church and its Bishops, 1700–1800*, vol. i, pp. 61–2.

a rule, there was only one tutor, (2) those founded 1691–1750, in which there were several tutors, and which were more " public " than the early ones, and (3) those founded much later, about 1750, which gave in addition to a professional training, a good general education to youths going into business.' Most of the students were preparing for the Dissenting Ministry, some for the Church, and many for the professions of medicine and law. Naturally, where a tutor was especially strong in a particular subject, the Academy would tend to specialize in that subject. In their day the Academies gave the best education to be had in this country. They stood ' immeasurably higher, as regards efficiency, than any other educational institutions '. Many evidences could be adduced to show that learning in Oxford and Cambridge in the eighteenth century was hardly more than a name. One is provided by no less a dignitary of the Established Church than Bishop Butler. In contrast with what he had previously received at Tewkesbury Academy, he found the education provided by Oriel College, Oxford, almost worthless. ' We are obliged ', he says, ' to misspend so much time in attending frivolous lectures and unintelligible disputations that I am quite tired out with such a disagreeable way of trifling.' [1] Overton, Abbey's fellow-historian of the Church, provides another : ' we have ', he says, ' the evidence of such different kinds of men as Swift, Defoe, Gray, Gibbon, Johnson, John Wesley, Lord Eldon, and Lord Chesterfield all agreeing on this point that both the great Universities were neglectful and inefficient in the performance of their proper work.' [2] Besides, whereas the Academies were

[1] Parker, *Dissenting Academies in England*, p. 130.
[2] Overton, *History of the Church of England in the Eighteenth Century*, vol. ii, p. 44.

famed as temples of virtue, the Universities were nurseries of vice. Abbey quotes Lord Campbell as saying that ' hard drinking ' was the ' chief recreation ' of Oxford, and Swift as inveighing against ' the idleness and the drinking ' there, and an anonymous writer as asserting of Cambridge that it had become so degenerate '·that the gentry of England begin to bethink themselves of acade- mies . . . to avoid a place where only poverty and the want of opportunity to be vicious, can secure from vice '.[1] Of the Academies' method of education we may take as illustrative Archbishop Secker's description of Samuel Jones's method at Tewkesbury Academy—that ' extra- ordinary place of education ' as he called it. Mr. Jones obliged his pupils to rise at five o'clock every morning, and always to speak Latin, except when they mixed with the family. ' We pass our time very agreeably betwixt study and conversation with our tutor, who is always ready to discourse freely of anything that is useful, and allows us either then, or at lecture, all imaginable liberty of making objections against his opinions, and prosecuting them as far as we can. In this and everything else, he shows himself so much a gentleman, and manifests so great an affection and tenderness for his pupils, as cannot but command respect and love.' [2]

Such was the general character of the education pro- vided in the Academies, of which Richard Price was a worthy product. It had brought him into contact with noble souls, it had surrounded him with an inspiring atmosphere. He entered upon life, therefore, a young man of first-class moral and intellectual equipment.

[1] Abbey, *The English Church and its Bishops, 1700–1800*, vol. i, p. 64.
[2] Letter from Secker to Isaac Watts, quoted in Wilson, *Dissenting Churches*, vol. i, p. 381 n.

CHAPTER II

Family chaplaincy in London — London pulpits — Presbyterian, and ‘ an acknowledged Arian ’ — Small inheritance — Marriage, and settlement in Hackney — Pastor of Stoke Newington — Moral Philosophy in England — *A Review of the Principal Questions in Morals* — brings immediate fame and gives its author a permanent place in the history of Philosophy — Price the anticipator of Kant.

UPON the completion of his education Richard Price, then twenty-one years old, accepted, on the advice of his uncle, the position of family chaplain to a Mr. Streatfield of Stoke Newington, which he filled until the death of his patron twelve years later. The post gave him ample opportunities for extending his reading and study, and afforded him a secure livelihood—two important considerations for him at that time. During his chaplaincy he also officiated occasionally at various Meeting-houses, and particularly to the congregations worshipping at the Old Jewry under the pastoral care of Dr. Samuel Chandler, one of the most renowned Dissenting ministers of the age. The congregation was a large and wealthy one of English Presbyterians. This religious body or denomination, which Price joined and within which he remained throughout his life, was a Nonconformist or Dissenting body which had originated with the ejectment of 1662. Presbyterian principles had, of course, been held by members and clergy of the Established Church for centuries, and have even been traced in the ancient British or Welsh Church.[1] Of the two thousand clergy who left the Church in 1662,

[1] Drysdale, *History of Presbyterianism in England*, pp. 8–10.

' about fifteen hundred, or three-fourths, allowed themselves to be designated Presbyterian ministers.' [1] The
other fourth comprised Independents and Baptists.
The English Presbyterians thus formed the bulk of the
Nonconformists, and ' the names Dissenter and Presbyterian were in some parts of the country synonymous.' [2]
The first ordination to perpetuate a Presbyterian ministry
outside the Established Church took place secretly in
Manchester in 1672—ten years after the ejectment.[3]
After the Revolution of 1688, or, more strictly, after
1689, when Nonconformist worship was recognized by law,
ordinations took place in public, and Meeting-houses for
the worship of Dissenting congregations generally and of
Presbyterian congregations in particular, were built. In
twenty-one years from 1689 there arose nearly a thousand
Meeting-houses, of which ' a full half ' belonged to the
Presbyterians. To the same body, too, belonged the
wealth. An illustration of the large resources of a Presbyterian congregation is provided by the Octagon Chapel,
Norwich, where the celebrated Dr. John Taylor, Dr.
William Enfield, and, late in the century, George Cadogan
Morgan, Price's nephew, ministered, which, in 1756, cost
above five thousand pounds to erect—an extremely large
sum in those days. As against the Independents, who
vested authority in the members of the Church, and whose
Church meeting enjoyed complete autonomy, the Presbyterians vested authority in the Minister, who ruled over
the Church, and who was ordained not by a Church or
Congregation but by a body of ordained ministers, and
often in private, the ordination service being always
extremely solemn and impressive. On this account,

---

[1] Drysdale, *History of Presbyterianism in England*, p. 389, n.
[2] Ibid., p. 441.   [3] Ibid., p. 456.

' Presbyterian ministers were, as a whole, much more
dignified and clerical in tone than their Independent
brethren.' [1] Whereas in the early part of the century
the Presbyterians were more numerous than the Independents, towards its close their positions were reversed,
a possible explanation being the more general deviation
from orthodoxy of the former. Thus, falling in numbers,
the Presbyterians rather fell also in wealth and worldly
respectability as the century advanced. Throughout the
century the denomination was marked by great partiality
for free inquiry, a remarkable degree of mental culture,
several of its ministers being most distinguished in science,
literature, and philosophy, and a passion for liberty, civil
and religious alike.[2] It appears that it was at the Old
Jewry that Price commenced his public ministry.[3] He
became assistant pastor to Chandler in 1744, that is, in
the same year that he commenced his chaplaincy with
Streatfield, but it is not certain in what year he relinquished the office. It is certain, however, that he did
not hold it long. The occasion of his severance from
it is said to have been ' a species of jealousy on the part
of Dr. Chandler, on account of the rising talents and
growing popularity of Mr. Price .' [4] This account is quite
compatible with another which makes Price's energy and
fervour in delivery an offence to Chandler, who rebuked
him for it, with the result that to avoid one extreme he
ran into the opposite extreme of a cold and lifeless
delivery, lost his popularity, and was relieved of his duties
by Chandler.[5] Price's energy and fervour were probably

[1] Ibid. p. 458.
[2] See Stoughton, *History of Religion in England,* vol. vi, pp. 296–
316, for details.
[3] Wilson, *Dissenting Churches,* vol. ii, p. 384.   [4] Ibid.
[5] Morgan, *Memoirs of the Life of the Rev. Richard Price,* pp. 11–12.

due partly to his experience of the Welsh ' hwyl ' and his own natural tendency, as a Welshman, to practise it, and partly to the influence of the torrential power of Howell Harris's oratory, which he had known in his student days at Chancefield. Be that as it may, Price harboured no ill-will towards Chandler, and we find him one of an influential number who, on Chandler's death, bought, with a view to their publication, some valuable critical Biblical notes in Latin which the latter had left. After severing his connexion with the Old Jewry, and while still residing with Streatfield, he officiated for a time at Edmonton.

Price's theological views took definite form early. He had given up the doctrine of the Trinity from quite an early age, and during his assistantship to Chandler, he was ' an acknowledged Arian '. A large number of tutors at the Academies and of pastors of Dissenting Churches, especially those belonging to the Presbyterian denomination, as well as clergymen of the Established Church, held Arian convictions before the close of the first half of the century, and Price was a substantial accession to their strength.

Streatfield, to whom Price had officiated as chaplain since 1744, died early in 1756. They had been very happy together, and Streatfield left Price a handsome legacy. Streatfield's house became the property of Lady Abney, the lady of the manor, widow of Sir Thomas Abney, the Nonconformist Sheriff, Lord Mayor, and ' father ' of the City of London, in whose house Isaac Watts had lived for many years. She thought highly of Price, and once accompanied him to Bridgend to see the beautiful country which he never failed to extol, going thither in a coach which it was found could not be accommodated in the town except in the street, where it had to be left day and night the object of curiosity and admiration.

In the same year that Price lost his patron he also lost his uncle, Samuel Price, who died in London on April 21, 1756, at the ripe age of 80 years. He had been active in the work of the ministry to the end. He was buried in Bunhill Fields, near the resting-place of Watts, with whom he had served so long. During a long life he had ' supported an exemplary character for probity and virtue '. He was a man of ' sound and solid sense ', a ' judicious, useful preacher ', and ' eminent for his gift in prayer '. He ' possessed great sagacity, was very able, faithful, and ready to advise and communicate his mind in serviceable hints and cautions to his friends '. His disposition was ' friendly and peaceable ', and he ' laid himself out to do good, in which he much delighted '.[1] He was highly esteemed by Watts, who referred to him in his will as his ' faithful friend and companion in the labours of the ministry ', and bequeathed to him a legacy ' as only a small testimony ' of his ' great affection for him on account of his services of love during the many harmonious years ' of their fellowship.[2] In his old age he had as assistants, first, Meredith Townshend, from 1742 to 1746, and second, Samuel Morton Savage, from 1747 to 1756, who also succeeded him in the pastorate. He did not publish much, the following sermons being all : ' To the Society who support the Morning Lecture at Little St. Helen's, August 1, 1724 ' ; ' To the Societies for Reformation of Manners, preached at Salters'-Hall, June 28, 1725 ' ; nine Sermons in the Bury Street Collection, 1735 ; ' A Charge at the Ordination of the Rev. John Angus, at Bishop's Stortford, 1748 ' ; and ' A Sermon on the Death of Dame Mary Abney, 1750 '. Samuel Price never married. He bequeathed most of his library for

---

[1] Wilson, *Dissenting Churches*, vol. i, p. 319.   [2] Ibid.

distribution among the ministers of Wales. Among other things he left his nephew, Richard, some property, including a house in Leadenhall Street. But the greater part of his fortune he left to his nephew John, Richard's brother, who had already inherited the Tynton estate. Placed by what he had been left by Streatfield and his uncle above pecuniary anxiety, Richard Price decided to set up a home of his own. On June 16, 1757, he married Miss Sarah Blundell, of Belgrave, Leicestershire, who lived at the time in London. She was a member of the Anglican Church, and remained so to the end of her life. The only daughter of one of those unfortunate speculators who had lost a large fortune in the notorious South Sea Bubble, she inherited only a remnant of her family's former wealth. This remnant consisted of a few thousand pounds and the house, situated at the corner of King Street, Cheapside, in the centre of London, in which she lived. By education, association, and religious views she was very different from the man she married, but he had fallen in love with her at first sight, and it is abundantly clear from every reference to their family life that his affection for her never waned. The fact that she became an invalid a few years after their marriage tended only to increase that affection during the remainder of their married life of nearly thirty years. In 1758, the year following his marriage, Price received a ' call ' to become morning and afternoon preacher to the congregation of English Presbyterians worshipping in the Meeting-house on the Green of Stoke Newington. His settlement here marks his full-time establishment in the public ministry, to which he gave of his best throughout a busy life. Of all the eminent and important roles he filled, none was allowed to interfere in the least with his pastoral work. For the first year after his marriage he lived in a narrow

street and noisy thoroughfare in Hackney. It was during
his residence here that, in 1758, at the age of thirty-five,
he published his first work. It was a treatise on Moral
Philosophy, entitled *A Review of the Principal Questions
and Difficulties in Morals.* He seems to have written it
during that period of greater leisure which the latter
portion of his chaplaincy afforded him, and the interval
between the end of his chaplaincy in 1756 and the commencement of his settled pastorate at Newington Green
in 1758, though, as he himself tells us, it was the fruit
of his studies from his earliest years. A second edition
was published in 1769, and a third, comprising the author's
' latest and maturest thoughts ', in 1787. It was written
in refutation of Hutcheson and Hume, and attracted the
immediate attention of the philosophical world. Hume,
in particular, noticed it. The attacks which had been
made on him lacked so much in civility that he admired
the replies which contained it. Such were those of Dr.
William Adams, Master of Pembroke College, Oxford,
and Archdeacon of Llandaff, and of Dr. John Douglas,
late Bishop of Salisbury, and, especially, the reply by
Price. The replies of the others showed neither the in-
sight nor the ability which that by Price showed, while
his certainly showed no less civility and candour than
theirs did. Samuel Rogers, the poet, who, as we shall see,
was brought up next door but one to Price, tells us that
Hume was desirous of being introduced to ' as many
of the persons who had written against him as could be
collected '.[1] Mr. Cadell, a well-known London publisher
of the period, arranged a meeting at Hume's request.
Price, Adams, and Douglas were of the party that dined
with Hume, by invitation, at Cadell's house in the Strand.

---

[1] G. H. Powell, *Table Talk of Samuel Rogers*, p. 67.

They passed their time ' in the utmost harmony and good humour '.[1] ' Dr. Price assured me ', says Rogers, ' that they were all delighted with David ' [2]—a testimony which accords well with that of General Fitzpatrick, who, having been ' much in the company of David Hume ' used ' always to speak of him as " a delicious creature " '.[3] The meeting proved to be only a first one for Price and Hume. Two of these meetings are worth our noting. One provides an interesting anecdote. Rogers tells us in his Commonplace Book that on one occasion as Price and Hume were discussing Rousseau—in many ways a very congenial spirit to both—' Dr. Price was told by Mr. Hume that when Rousseau came with him to England he suspected that he was seduced over to be poisoned ; and on the way one night, as they lay in separate rooms divided by a single partition, Rousseau heard Mr. Hume cry out in his sleep " I've got you Rousseau ; I've got you ! " Rousseau left him and went off into Derbyshire, where he took it into his head that the people of England had entered into a conspiracy against him, and wrote up to the minister for a guard to escort him out of the kingdom. Hume, with much difficulty, prevailed on the king to grant Rousseau a pension of a hundred pounds a year, but when he was informed of it he spurned it as an affront.' [4] The other meeting shows the interest Price and Hume took in each other's philosophical teaching. During one of Hume's several visits to Price at his house in Newington Green, he ' candidly acknowledged that on one point Mr. Price had succeeded in convincing him that his arguments were inconclusive '.[5] It is unfortunate that there is no clue as to what that point was.

[1] Morgan, *Memoirs*, p. 17.   [2] Powell, *Table Talk*, p. 67.
[3] Ibid.   [4] Clayden, *Early Life of Samuel Rogers*, p. 303.
[5] Morgan, *Memoirs*, p. 17.

The two writers by whom Price is most influenced in his moral theory are Butler and Clarke. Joseph Butler, Bishop of Durham, had published his *Analogy of Religion* in 1736, and his *Fifteen Sermons*, most of which dealt almost wholly with questions of moral philosophy, ten years before. We noticed Price, then a boy in his teens, reading the *Analogy* when on his way, over snow-clad mountains, from the Talgarth Academy to Bridgend. Of that work Price, late in his life, says, ' I reckon it happy for me that this book was one of the first that fell into my hands. It taught me the proper mode of reasoning on moral and religious subjects, and particularly the importance of paying a due regard to the imperfection of human knowledge.' [1] In the *Review* itself he refers to Butler as ' an incomparable writer '. ' Next to *his* works ', he continues, ' I have always been an admirer of the writings of Dr. Clarke '.[2] Price then goes on to make an extremely significant statement. Kant, it is well known, was very greatly indebted to Hume, whom he opposed. It has not been known, however, that Price also was indebted to him, and in exactly the same way. Yet that is the truth. Kant's words are well known : ' I freely admit that it was David Hume's reminder, which, many years ago, first aroused me from my dogmatic slumber, and gave my investigations in the field of speculative philosophy a new direction.' [3] Price, in very similar words, says ' And I cannot help adding, however strange it may seem, that I owe much to the philosophical writings of Mr. Hume, which I . . . studied early in life. Though an enemy to his scepticism, I have profited by it. By attacking, with great ability, every principle of truth and reason, he put

---

[1] Price's *Observations on the Importance of the American Revolution* ; Preface.

[2] Ibid.   [3] *Prolegomena*, Introd.

me upon examining the ground upon which I stood, and taught me not hastily to take anything for granted.' [1] Now, whereas formerly the awakening influence of Hume on Kant was referred to the period between 1762 and 1766, Paulsen, who questioned the correctness of this, suggested a later date, 1769.[2]   Latterly, however, the tendency has been to place the date still later.   Royce, following Erdmann, accepts as most probable ' the years immediately following 1772 '.[3]   On the other hand, the date of Price's awakening by Hume falls ' early in life ' and belongs, no doubt, to the years of his studentship at Chancefield, where he was reading Butler ; if not, indeed, to the years of his studies at Pentwyn, where he began reading Clarke.   That is, it falls not later than 1744, and, it may be, as early as 1735.   It is clear, therefore, that Price had not only come under Hume's influence much earlier than Kant, but that he had even published his answer in the *Review* several years before Kant came under Hume's influence, and more than twenty years before Kant published his answer in 1781 [4] and 1785,[5] the latter date being that of his first work on Moral Philosophy.

To be fully appreciated, the *Review* must be read in the light of the philosophical controversies of the period, for it was they that called it forth, and it was by way of answer to their fundamental questions that it was conceived.   But though the work is thus polemical, it is

[1] Price's *Observations on the Importance of the American Revolution* ; Preface.

[2] See discussion in *Immanuel Kant, his Life and Doctrine*, pp. 93 ff., 97 ff.

[3] Royce, *The Spirit of Modern Philosophy*, pp. 125–6.

[4] *Critique of Pure Reason.*

[5] *Fundamental Principles of the Metaphysic of Morals.*

definitely constructive, and on that account, as well as
on account of its anticipating an epoch-making philosophy
which was to follow, it must be regarded as a permanent
contribution to philosophical thought and a classic of the
science to which it belongs.

The eighteenth century had inherited from the seventeenth certain moral problems to which very different
solutions were offered, and around which, therefore, a
discussion ranged itself. The questions were very old,
but they were now discussed for the first time in Britain.
Briefly, they were : Whence do we derive the ideas of
right and wrong ? By what power are we able to know
right and wrong ? What are right and wrong ? Those
who agree about the answer to one of these questions might
differ about the answer to another of them. Nor were the
questions always considered apart. Besides, one writer
would make one of these the main question ; another,
another. The writers of the period, therefore, might be
variously classified, the classification depending upon
which of these questions would be taken as the dividing
one. The most useful classification is that which rests
upon the answers given to the question of the Moral
Faculty. Those answers fall in the main into two groups :
those which say that we know the right by a kind of
feeling, which is sometimes called a ' moral sense ', and
those which say that we know it by the intellect. Such
a classification gives us two schools of ethical thought,
commonly referred to as the ' Sentimental ' and the ' Intellectual ', or the ' Moral Sense ' and the ' Rational '
schools. Those who identify the moral faculty with
feeling or sense, generally find the criterion of right and
wrong in the tendency of action to produce or not produce
pleasure. Those who identify the moral faculty with
intellect or reason, generally hold the criterion of right

and wrong to be not the tendency of an action to produce or not produce an effect outside itself, but the direct, immediate perception of the action as right or wrong by us ; that is, they hold that we know the right by ' intuition ', and that we cannot define it by referring it to anything else. Both schools have to meet formidable objections. The former have the obvious difficulty, to speak of no others, of satisfactorily apportioning pleasure to self and others. The latter have to explain the wide divergence of opinions and customs with regard to right and wrong the world over, and throughout the ages. This classification, however, must not be taken to mean that writers of one school have no point in common with writers of the other, nor that all who took part in the controversy can be easily classed with either school. Butler is a notable case in point. He is variously interpreted—as a sentimentalist and as an intellectualist—by good authorities. Nevertheless, the classification is, broadly speaking, well based, and serves to bring out the significance of the chief works of the period. The sentimental or ' moral sense ' school is best represented by the Earl of Shaftesbury, Francis Hutcheson, and David Hume ; the intellectual or rational school by Ralph Cudworth, Samuel Clarke, and Richard Price. Soon after its publication, Price's *Review* ' was acknowledged, by all capable of appreciating its value, to be the most able defence ' of the principles of the intellectual school ' in the English language '.[1] And it remains to this day the best exposition of the moral theory which it sets forth.

To summarize the argument of the *Review* is not our purpose here. Its fundamental points, however, especially in so far as they show Price as the anticipator of Kant,

----

[1] Dr. Abraham Rees, *Life of Dr. Price*, in Dr. Rees's *Cyclopedia*.

may be very briefly indicated. The power within us that perceives the distinctions of right and wrong is the understanding.[1] This, Price holds, has two acts, intuition and deduction, and he invariably uses the term as denoting the former.[2] As against the philosophy of Locke, which really underlay the ethical thought of the moral sense school, he contends that the understanding is itself a source of new ideas,[3] in morals as in other fields, a view which Kant also held later. Though Price does not build upon it, he does clearly lay down the distinction between theoretical and practical reason,[4] a distinction which Kant, though differing from Price in distinguishing between reason and understanding, makes one of the premises of his great system. Combating the tendency of the opposite school to reduce right to pleasure, or utility, and again anticipating Kant, Price holds that right is irresolvable ; it is a simple and ultimate idea that cannot be analysed into anything else.[5] It is perceived by the intuitive reason. Moral distinctions, as Kant also would say, do not depend upon anything arbitrary ; they are distinctions in the natures of things ; [6] they are absolute, immutable, and eternal.[7] Price is as uncompromising as Kant in not admitting an action to be right because it gives pleasure. Further, it must be recognized that he is on far more tenable ground than Kant is when the latter refuses to give any place whatsoever to pleasurable feeling in relation to right, and so refuses to regard any action which pleases as right. Price both corrects those whom he opposes, who, wrongly, make pleasure a condition precedent of right; and avoids the error of his successor Kant, who, equally wrongly, insists that right action must

[1] *Review*, p. 15.   [2] Ibid., p. 17 n.   [3] Ibid., p. 16, 49.
[4] Ibid., pp. 386–7.   [5] Ibid., pp. 57–8.   [6] Ibid., pp. 139, 411.
[7] Ibid., pp. 74, 144, 411, 460.

necessarily be devoid of pleasure. He makes pleasure the attendant effect or concomitant of right action.[1] The position, however, which gives Price still greater eminence is his thorough-going insistence upon the obligatory nature of the moral law. Obligation to action and rightness of action are, for him, concomitant and identical.[2] Rectitude is a law as well as a rule; it not only directs but binds all as far as it is perceived. Kant occupied precisely the same position nearly thirty years later. His ' categorical imperative ' is an almost exact re-assertion of Price's conception, though Kant alone used that term. Moreover, the conception is a central one in the theory of each. The demands of the moral law are supreme and ultimate. Fulfilment of them presupposes, in addition to reason, liberty,[3] and intention,[4] both of which Kant's system likewise requires. Price's exposition of liberty is clear and vigorous, and it is well that we should notice here that his love of liberty dominates, and so explains, all his subsequent activities, and that his life is in fact the realization of a philosophy. To this moral law, the fulfilment of which is made possible by liberty, reason, and intention, Price has given noble expression in a passage which deserves to become a classic expression of what Kant called the ' Categorical Imperative ' : ' Rectitude, then, or Virtue, is a Law. And it is the first and supreme law, to which all other laws owe their force, on which they depend, and in virtue of which alone they oblige. It is an universal Law. The whole creation is ruled by it ; under it men and all rational beings subsist. It is the source and guide of all the actions of the Deity himself, and on it his throne and government are founded. It is

[1] *Review*, pp. 63, 91, 118.   [2] Ibid., pp. 74 n., 78, 168–81.
[3] Ibid., pp. 305 ff.   [4] Ibid., 310 ff.

an unalterable and indispensable Law. The repeal, suspension, or even relaxation of it, once for a moment, in any part of the universe, cannot be conceived without a contradiction. Other laws have had a date ; a time when they were enacted and became of force. They are confined to particular places, rest on precarious foundations, may lose their vigour, grow obsolete with time, and become useless and neglected. Nothing like this can be true of this law. It has no date. It never was made nor enacted. It is prior to all things. It is self-valid and self-originated ; and must for ever retain its usefulness and vigour, without the possibility of diminution or abatement. It is coeval with eternity ; as unalterable as necessary, everlasting truth ; as independent as the existence of God ; and as sacred and awful as his nature and perfections. The authority it possesses is native and essential to it, underived and absolute. It is superior to all other authority, and the basis and parent of all other authority. It is indeed self-evident that, properly speaking, there is no other authority ; nothing else that can claim our obedience, or that ought to guide and rule heaven and earth. It is, in short, the one authority in nature, the same in all times and in all places ; or, in one word, the Divine authority.'[1] Kant himself nowhere clothes his imperative with more imperious sovereignty.

Included in the third edition of the *Review*, Price has ' A Dissertation on the Being and Attributes of the Deity '. The method of argument is identical in both. Price holds that our conviction of the existence of a Maker of the world does not depend upon ' reasonings and deductions ', but is ' the effect of immediate and irresistible perception '.[2] It is the Understanding, understood as Intuitive Reason, that informs us of the existence of God.

[1] *Review*, pp. 178–9.　　　　　　　[2] Ibid., p. 489.

CHAPTER III

Removal from Hackney to Newington Green — Acquaintance of Franklin and Priestley — Wife becomes an invalid — Despondency, and the refusal of a Tutorship in Academy and the editorship of Newton's works — Evening preacher in Poor Jewry Lane — Thoughts of failure in the ministry — Membership of Dr. Daniel Williams's Trust — Papers to the Royal Society — Election to ' F.R.S. ' — *Four Dissertations* — Defence of Miracles against David Hume — Acquaintance of Lord Shelburne and Lord Lyttelton — ' D.D.' from Aberdeen — Morning preacher at the Gravel Pit, Hackney, retaining also Stoke Newington — Noted members of latter congregation — William Morgan.

AFTER a year's residence in Hackney, Price removed, in the middle of 1758, to Stoke Newington, in order to be nearer his congregation. Stoke Newington was then a suburban village, in a well-wooded region, with a population of less than a thousand, many of whom were retired statesmen and merchantmen. It was noted for its Dissent, several celebrities of that persuasion living there. During the first year of his residence there, he gave himself up almost entirely to the work of the ministry, lamenting as a trifling waste of time the few hours which he spent in the study of philosophy and mathematics and in the harmless relaxation of visiting his friends, other than those who were members of his congregation. Amongst his friends at this time, in addition to those we have noted, were scientists like John Canton, F.R.S., Benjamin Franklin, F.R.S., and Joseph Priestley, also soon to become a F.R.S. Canton, a native of Stroud, was a successful schoolmaster in London, and became famous by his work on the compressibility of water, for which he was awarded the gold medal of the Royal Society, and in the composition of which Price paid him helpful attention.   Franklin was already a man of great fame.   He had been in England since July 27, 1757, having come over to represent the American colonies on the vexed question of taxation.   Soon after his arrival he formed a close friendship with Price, who was twenty years his junior ;   and they remained on terms of the closest friendship until death parted them, Price surviving Franklin by a year.   Joseph Priestley, who had joined the staff of the Dissenting Academy which had been opened at Warrington in 1757, had just begun his practice of visiting London for a month every year, and had made the acquaintance of Canton and Franklin, as well as of Price. Priestley, like Franklin, became Price's intimate and lasting friend.   The three cherished for one another the greatest affection and respect for a period of over thirty years, at the end of which Priestley, who was ten years younger than Price, mourned the loss of both, he living for many years longer, only to suffer, however, the effects of disgraceful intolerance and persecution.[1]

The early years at Newington Green were for Price marked by considerable despondency.   The illness of his wife, which left her an invalid for the rest of her life, and the indifference of his own health, were causes of this. But he kept his troubles to himself and did not allow them to prevent him from maintaining in society the appearance of his usual cheerfulness.   His mind being disposed to piety from his youth, he was now extra-ordinarily impressed with the importance of religion, and came to regard the pursuit of all subjects not directly connected with it as vain and trifling.   During those years

[1] See p. 141.

he rejected two important offers. One, made to him in November 1762, was to become a tutor in his old Academy, which was being removed from Well-close Square to Hoxton. Both Dr. Andrew Kippis and Dr. Abraham Rees, with whom, especially the former, Price enjoyed a lifelong friendship, were then on its staff. The other was an offer from the booksellers to edit the works of Sir Isaac Newton. This would have been a very congenial task for him, for he had the greatest admiration for the great friend of his old tutor. He felt that he must give himself entirely to his pulpit. But he also refused an invitation to the pastorate of Lewin's Mead, Bristol, one of the most important Presbyterian congregations outside London. Price chose to remain in London. In 1763, he became evening preacher to the congregation of English Presbyterians in Poor Jewry Lane. In 1762, Dr. Benson, who had been assisted by Ebenezer Radcliffe, retired from the Lane pastorate, being succeeded by his assistant. Benson had been evening preacher and Radcliffe morning preacher, and when the latter succeeded to the pastorate he continued to occupy the morning pulpit, so that it was the evening pulpit left vacant by Benson which Price filled in the capacity of assistant to Radcliffe. On his acceptance of this office, Price gave up the afternoon service at Newington Green. Both in the morning service at the latter place, which he still retained, and in the evening service at Poor Jewry Lane, the congregations were very small. He officiated at the Lane for seven years. Even at the time of Dr. Lardner and Dr. Benson, Radcliffe's eminent predecessors in the pastorate, the church was in a very low state. The decrease in the membership continued, and in 1774, when Dr. Calder had followed Price as assistant, the Society was dissolved. Whether it had been the paucity of his hearers, or his own low spirits which inclined him in that direction, Price had become so discouraged that he even contemplated renouncing the ministry. There does not seem to be any justification for his believing, if he really did believe, that he lacked effectiveness in the pulpit. And it is well that in spite of discouragement he held fast to the belief that the saving of souls and the amelioration of men required all his talents. This faith not only kept him in the ministry but enabled him to take a wider view of the legitimate use of both his talents and his time. Price, in fact, already stood high in the councils of his brother ministers. In 1761, he was elected a member of Dr. Daniel Williams's Trust, an office he held until his death.[1] Daniel Williams, a native of Wrexham, who had sat under the preaching of Walter Cradoc there, and was, like Samuel Jones, Brynllywarch, a friend of Baxter, was one of the founders of the Presbyterian Fund. He left a large estate, which he had acquired by marriage, in trust for the education of students for the Christian ministry, the assistance of preachers of the Word, the relief of ministers' widows, the distribution of books, the instruction of children, and the maintenance of a public library.[2] 'Dr. Williams's Library' is now one of the best known in the country. Ever since its foundation, the Trust has been managed by ministers and laymen of the highest standing in the Presbyterian denomination. Both from the general purpose of the Trust, and from its special patronage of Wales,[3] Price found its administration very congenial work.

The death of a mathematician friend was the occasion of setting Price on a line of mathematical inquiry that

---

[1] Jeremy, *The Presbyterian Fund Board, and Dr. Daniel Williams' Trust*, p. 150.

[2] Ibid., p. ix.   [3] Ibid., p. 34.

proved most fruitful. The Rev. Thomas Bayes, F.R.S., minister of the Presbyterian Church in Tunbridge Wells, died on April 17, 1761. His mathematical skill had been praised by no less a person than William Whiston, Newton's successor at Cambridge. He left a considerable amount of work in manuscript, and Price, as a friend and an accomplished mathematician, was asked to examine it. He found that Bayes had stated, but had only imperfectly solved, a problem in the Doctrine of Chances, and he realized at once that its solution was most desirable and would be of far-reaching importance. The problem was : ' Given the number of times an unknown event has happened and failed, required the chance that the probability of its happening in a single trial lies somewhere between any two degrees of probability that may be named.' In 1763 he offered a solution of it in a letter to his friend Canton, who was so impressed with it that he offered it to the Royal Society. In the same year it was published in the Society's *Philosophical Transactions*. In the following year, Price offered the Society an improved solution, which also was published in the *Transactions*. These papers earned for Price the Fellowship of the Royal Society, to which he was elected on December 5, 1765.[1] He appreciated the honour very highly, and especially the increased facilities it would give him of associating with the leading mathematicians and scientists of the day.

Price now applied himself more freely to his favourite subjects. He decided to publish the Sermons he had preached on the subject of Prayer. They were recast into the form of a treatise, and with them were included three

[1] Extract Minute and date kindly supplied by the Assistant Secretary, Royal Society.

other treatises : ' On Providence ', ' On the Junction of Virtuous Men in a Heavenly State ', and ' Historical Evidence and Miracles '. They were published under the title *Four Dissertations*, in 1767. One of these subjects, that of Miracles, had occupied his attention at intervals for more than seven years, and his Dissertation on it is much the most important of the four. Nearly twenty years before, in 1748, David Hume had written an *Essay on Miracles* with the object of disproving their credibility. It was against Hume's Essay that Price's Treatise was directed. It had been read to friends, who had all recommended its publication. In his treatment of the subject he made use of a principle he had previously proved in his Papers on the Doctrine of Chances. It was characteristic of Price that, having expressed himself improperly, as he thought, in this Dissertation, he made, on his sending a copy of his book to Hume, a sincere apology therefor, and promised that should there be a subsequent edition, that form of expression should not appear in it. He received from Hume a very flattering letter which he regarded more as a matter of civility than as a proof of his having wrought any change in Hume's sentiments. When another edition did appear, Price fulfilled his promise and sent a corrected copy to Hume, for which he immediately received an acknowledgement expressing Hume's ' wonder at such scrupulosity ' in one of Price's profession. The *Four Dissertations* brought Price another coveted distinction. The Degree of Doctor of Divinity was conferred upon him by the Marischal College, Aberdeen, on August 7, 1767.[1] Several others had written replies to

[1] Extract Minute and date kindly supplied by the Librarian, The University, Aberdeen. Morgan erroneously states in the *Memoirs*, p. 42, that the degree was obtained from Glasgow, and in 1769. A note kindly supplied by the Registrar, The University, Glasgow,

Hume, notably Dr. William Adams, Master of Pembroke College, Oxford, Archdeacon of Llandaff, and a valued friend of Price ; Dr. John Douglas, Bishop of Salisbury ; and Dr. George Campbell, Principal of the Marischal College, Aberdeen, whose *Dissertation on Miracles* had attracted some attention. The *Four Dissertations* were the means of their author's making the acquaintance, in 1769, of the Earl of Shelburne, and, soon afterwards, of Lord Lyttelton. Shelburne, who had then newly lost his wife, was recommended by Mrs. Montague, the famous ' blue-stocking ', who had for some years been well acquainted with Price, to read the Dissertations on ' Providence ' and on ' The Virtuous and a Future State '. He was so highly pleased with them that he immediately expressed a wish to be introduced to the author. A day was accordingly appointed for a meeting at Price's house. Shelburne, struck with the unaffected simplicity of his new acquaintance, soon repeated his visit. Thus began an acquaintance which ripened into the most intimate friendship and the closest mutual confidence. Lord Lyttelton, who had himself published an excellent ' Essay on the Conversion of St. Paul ', also visited Price at his home, ' to talk with one of the clearest thinkers of the age on the transcendent themes in which he felt so profound an interest ' ; [1] but their acquaintance lasted

makes it clear that Price's name does not appear in that University's records.

Both J. M. Mitchell, in his article on Price in the *Encyclopædia Britannica*, 11th ed., 1910–11, and Professor T. Fowler, President of Corpus Christi, Oxford, in his articles in the *Encyclopædia Britannica*, 9th and 10th eds., repeat the double error as regards both University and date. Fowler has the error also in his article in the *Dictionary of National Biography*, 1896.

[1] Clayden, *The Early Life of Samuel Rogers*, p. 31.

only a few years owing to the death of Lyttelton in 1773.
Price's argument for Providence follows two lines : that
of the Divine perfections, and that of the constitution of
the world.   In the idea of perfection are implied infinite
power, wisdom, and goodness ; and in these is implied
providence.   ' A God without a Providence is a contradiction.' [1]   And there is a plan or constitution of nature by
which beings are provided for, and an influence of the
Deity constantly exerted to maintain this constitution.
But what of the irregularities and evils, natural and
moral, which exist ?   Evil is either a reality or only an
appearance due to our ignorance.   In the former case,
it arises from a ' *want* of wisdom ' ; in the latter, from an
' *infinity* of wisdom ', in the Deity.   The former is inad-
missible ; the latter is ' in the highest degree easy, natural,
and obvious '.[2]   It is significant that the chief difficulties
lie just where we might expect them—not in the natural
world which ' lies more or less in one view before us ', but
in the moral world, which ' must be of inconceivable extent
as to duration as well as to place '.[3]   Nor is Providence to
be understood as destructive of free agency ; on the
contrary, it is quite consistent with the completest liberty.[4]
Prayer, for Price, is ' so inseparably connected with the
love of God in the soul that they are almost the same '.
More fully he defines it as ' the exercise of our highest
affections on their highest object, and the intercourse of
our minds with uncreated and sovereign goodness '.[5]   It
consists of four parts : an ' acknowledgement of our dependence, and of the Divine perfections and sovereignty ' ;
' thankfulness for the mercies we have received ' ; ' a
penitential confession of what we have done amiss ' [6] ; and

[1] *Four Dissertations*, p. 6.   [2] Ibid., p. 107.
[3] Ibid., p. 110.   [4] Ibid., pp. 94–5.
[5] Ibid., p. 246.   [6] Ibid., p. 198.

an ' expression of our desires of favour for ourselves and others '.[1] What is the justification of prayer ? Its fitness ' is immediately perceived by the lowest as well as the highest understanding '. No words can make it plainer than it must appear by its own light. As to a Future State, Price believes, not in *a* future state merely, but that there are periods of existences before us. Any future state will be one in which ' present inequalities will be set right and a suitable distinction made between good and bad men '. We shall then recover ' the greater part if not the whole of our present consciousness '. Our state will be ' an ascent in dignity and bliss which will never come to an end ', for we have ' latent powers ' which it is ' the business of eternity to evolve '. The ' Dissertation on Miracles ', in answer to Hume, takes the form of an examination of the question of the regard due to testimony when its reports do not agree with experience. Hume's denial that any regard is due to it formed the pith of his objection to miracles. Price urges that the ground of the regard we pay to human testimony is plainly not experience only. ' We feel in ourselves that a regard to truth is one principle in human nature.' The greatest part of experience is merely the report of testimony. To see how fallacious is Hume's assertion that ' no testimony should even gain credit to an event unless it is more extraordinary that it should be false than that the event should have happened ', we need ' only consider the degree of improbability which there is against almost all the most common facts, independently of the evidence of testimony for them '. On Hume's principle, were we to be eye-witnesses of anything quite new to us, we would be wrong in believing the reality of it, inasmuch as it would be

<hr>

[1] *Four Dissertations*, p. 354.

' receiving a fact upon evidence the falsehood of which would be less uncommon than the fact itself '. Whence follows, Price points out, the natural conclusion, to which Hume's philosophy leads, that ' we have no reason for believing the existence of any external objects or the reality of anything we hear, see, or feel, except as a mode of perception in our minds '—which is pure scepticism.[1]

Having officiated for about twelve years as morning preacher at Newington Green, where the congregation had always been very small, Price accepted, in 1770, the office of morning preacher at the Gravel Pit Meeting-house, Hackney. The congregation here, which, again, was one of English Presbyterians, was considerably larger than that at the former place. He remained pastor to the Gravel Pit congregation to the end of his life. Price, it may be noted, believed, as his friends Priestley and Lindsey did, that ministers should retire at the age of 70.[2] He, however, did not live to serve to the limit he was laying down. He did not sever his connexion with Newington Green when he associated himself with the Gravel Pit, but exchanged the morning for the evening service there, resigning the office of evening preacher at Poor Jewry Lane in order to do so. He continued to live at Newington Green. There he had as neighbour Thomas Rogers, father of the poet Samuel Rogers, who lived next door but one to him. The Rogers family, including the boy Samuel, were ' regular in their attendance '[3] at the Meeting-house on the Green, and ' in the next pew to them sat Mary Wollstonecraft ',[4] then a girl, but destined to become

[1] Ibid., pp. 433–4.
[2] Belsham, *Memoirs of Lindsey*, p. 266.
[3] Clayden, *Early Life of Samuel Rogers*, p. 29.
[4] Ibid.

' the one woman of genius who belonged to the English revolutionary circle ' ;[1] who was one of the first, if not actually the first, to preach the doctrine of the equality of the sexes ; who, further, was to write, towards the very end of the century, ' one of the books which belong to the spiritual foundations of the next century ' ;[2] and the daughter of whose marriage with the equally famous revolutionary, William Godwin, became the wife of the poet Shelley.

Living with Price was his nephew, William Morgan, the son of his sister Sarah. She had, in 1744, become the second wife of William Morgan, of Tyla Coch, near Bridgend. William Morgan, senior, who had ' inherited Tyla Coch by female descent from the Cadogans who had once ruled over the whole valley of the Rhondda ', was then practising as a doctor in Bridgend, having succeeded Dr. Richards, Price's grandfather.[3] The youth was pursuing his studies in London for his father's profession, and Price, who had no children, appreciated his company, and found ' much satisfaction in my nephew Billy '. Nor was the young nephew unappreciative of the society of his ' heavenly uncle ', as he called him. In the summer of 1772, William Morgan, senior, died suddenly, having only the day before dined at Dunraven Castle ' where he had long been welcomed as a doctor and a friend '.[4] There had always been the most thorough congeniality between Price and the Morgans. He was invariably received with delight by them in their home at Newcastle, Bridgend, when he made his summer visit to his native county.[5] Price was about to pay a visit to Lord Shelburne

---

[1] Brailsford, *Shelley, Godwin, and their Circle*, H. U. L., p. 147.

[2] Ibid., pp. 147–8.

[3] Williams, *A Welsh Family*, pp. 1–2.

[4] Ibid., p. 35. [5] Ibid., p. 11.

at Calne, the latter's seat in Wiltshire, when he heard of his brother-in-law's death. Feeling that the greatest comfort he could give his widowed sister was to be near her, he resolved to go on from Calne. Mrs. Morgan had every reason to rely on her brother for all possible support and consolation, and her children found in him a father. When leaving London for Bridgend to carry out his father's wish that he should succeed him in the practice there and be a comfort to his mother, William Morgan, junior, lamented the ' sad and gloomy prospect ' of leaving ' my heavenly-minded friends at Newington Green, among whom such unbounded love reigns '. Though he felt ' assured of a constant friend ' in his mother he could not but tell her : ' The thought of separating from Dr. Price damps every pleasure and checks the joy I should otherwise feel at the prospect of returning home.' [1] It was not long, however, before the young man was back with his uncle in London, seeking his advice, much as Price himself, more than twenty years before, had sought the advice of *his* uncle. Even before William Morgan, senior, died, a competitor for his practice had appeared in Bridgend in the person of Jenkin Williams, the newly-qualified son of a neighbour who farmed Stormy. Morgan, senior, it seems, had not much approved of the gay dress of his young rival, and feared that the good-looking young doctor with his tall person would turn the heads of his daughters. ' Girls,' he would say, ' don't lose your hearts to this young coxcomb, with his fine gold-laced hat.' The event he had so much feared, however, came to pass in the year following his death. Soon after young Morgan took up his father's practice, Jenkin Williams married, in 1773, his sister, Kitty. This event proved a turning-

[1] Ibid., pp. 28, 29.

E

point in young Morgan's life, for rather than compete with his brother-in-law he gave up his practice and returned to London. He was young and able, and his uncle soon found an opportunity not only to employ him profitably, but to set him on a new and successful career.

CHAPTER IV

'Bubble' insurance societies — Price examines the question of annuities — 'Observations on the Expectation of Lives' — 'Observations on the values of reversions depending on Survivorships' — which corrects an error of De Moivre — *Observations on Reversionary Payments* — which bursts the 'bubbles' — The Equitable Society and 'Actuary Morgan' — Price the founder of Life Insurance — *Reversionary Payments* and schemes for old age — Price's scheme to the House of Commons — Price the father of Old Age Pensions — *Appeal to the Public on the National Debt* — Price influences French finance — The population of the kingdom — Agitation for religious freedom — First 'Unitarian' periodical — First 'Unitarian' Chapel — London parties.

PRICE had for some time been regarded as a mathematician of the front rank, and an authority on financial questions. An event now occurred which gave him occasion for showing further his great powers in the application of mathematics to social and political problems. We are to-day so familiar with the working of life-insurance and of old-age pensions that we are apt to forget that the practice of neither goes back very far, that of the latter being quite recent. What is the history of life insurance, and what point had it reached in Price's day ? We are told [1] that ' guesses at the probable length of life for the purpose of valuing or commuting life-estates, leases or annuities were made even by the ancients ', and that ' crude estimates of the number of years' purchase such interests are worth occur in Roman law and in medieval writings '. In the sixteenth century

---

[1] Gow, Art. *Encycl. Brit.*, 11th ed., whence the quotations in this paragraph.

there appeared *The Cambridge Tables for renewing the Leases and purchasing Liens,* ' a standard work in England, with the certificate of Sir Isaac Newton to its accuracy '. But in this table ' no distinction of ages was recognized ', and its results are ' worthless '. The position, therefore, was that ' the foremost minds of the world had as yet no apprehension of a true method of reasoning on the subject '. Governments were soon tempted to speculate in the matter, the sale of annuities being considered a convenient method of discounting future revenues. This speculation led Dr. Edmund Halley, the eminent mathematician and astronomer, to examine the subject. In 1693 he constructed a table of mortality based on the registers of Breslau. It is this table that first recognizes the two essential factors in annuity values : compound interest and the probability of life. Throughout the eighteenth century ' the customary treatment of life annuities was as chaotic and fanciful as before, though some writers of eminence, most notably Dr. Thomas Simpson of London (1752) treated the theory of the subject with great intelligence '. De Moivre, also, the renowned French Protestant mathematician, who, during his residence in England was appointed judge in a mathematical controversy between Newton and Leibnitz, constructed a table about 1750, but based it ' on a hypothesis of his own, and not on known facts '. Such, we understand on the best authority, was the state of the theory and practice of life insurance in Price's day.

Price had entered upon a study of the subject. The papers by him published in the *Philosophical Transactions* dealt with a problem fundamental to life insurance. His contribution in them consisted not alone in the mere solution of the problem, but also in his grasping the full significance of a solution. He had also in a letter to his friend, Benjamin Franklin, offered *Observations on the Expectations of Lives*, which was read to the Royal Society on April 27, 1769, and published in the *Transactions* for that year. Again, he had published in the *Transactions* for the following year *Observations on the proper method of calculating the values of reversions depending on survivorships*, in the preparation of which he discovered and corrected serious defects in De Moivre's tables relative to the value of Joint Lives. It is said that so great was his concentration on the work that his hair grew white in parts as a consequence.

The practice of insurance as a *business* did not begin until the middle of the eighteenth century, and even then it was ' little understood '.[1] Insurance societies were being formed, however, and the public were easily persuaded to subscribe to them.[2] Some had as their object the provision of annuities for survivors, others, annuities for old age, while others covered both survivorships and old age. Price discovered that they were all based on plans ' alike improper and insufficient '. Many of these, no doubt, had been devised in ignorance, and were based on very incorrect data ; but there was room to believe that some of them arose from dishonest motives. In either case the evil consequences were serious, for the savings of many long years were lost in them. A few years before 1771, ' many gentlemen of the first eminence in the law formed themselves into a Society for providing

[1] William Morgan's edition of Price's work on *Annuities*, two vols., 7th ed., 1812, Introd.

[2] Richard Price, *Reversionary Payments*, 3rd ed., 1773, Preface to the 1st ed. All the facts and quotations in this section, unless otherwise denoted, are from Price's *Reversionary Payments*, which is mentioned in the text further on. The edition used is the 3rd, 1773, which contains also the Preface to the 1st ed.

annuities for the widows of all such persons in judicial offices, barristers, civilians, and solicitors, as should choose to become members. A plan was agreed upon and printed, but, some doubts happening to arise with respect to it, the directors resolved to ask the opinion and advice of three gentlemen, well known for their skill in calculation '. ' This ', continues Price, ' occasioned a further reference to me ; and the issue was, that the plan being found to be insufficient, the whole design was laid aside '. An extended examination led Price to a like conclusion with regard to other societies. ' Finding therefore ', says he, ' that the public wanted information on the subject, I was led to undertake this work '. The work was his *Observations on Reversionary Payments*. It was published in 1771 and dedicated to the Earl of Shelburne. A design which its author at first thought would give him little trouble carried him far into a very wide field of inquiry, and engaged him in calculations that took up much time and labour. He felt, however, that he would be sufficiently rewarded should his work prove to be the means of preventing any part of that distress which he saw was bound to follow the carrying out of the several insecure schemes then existing. Price's claim, a claim that was abundantly justified, was that ' in this work he proved the inadequateness of those plans by undeniable facts and mathematical demonstration ' ; and, more important still, that he gave ' an account of some of the best plans that are consistent with a sufficient probability of permanence and success ', so that ' should any of these societies determine to reform themselves, or should any institutions of the same kind be hereafter published, they will here find direction and assistance '. It is the simple truth that Price's *Reversionary Payments* placed the practice of insurance, for the first time in history, on a reliable basis

by providing it with a sound mathematical foundation.
While ' to Dr. Halley, Mr. De Moivre, and Mr. Thomas
Simpson, and particularly to the latter, we owe the first
rudiments and improvements of this science ', we must
remember that ' for the more accurate knowledge of it we
are indebted to Dr. Price '.[1]

The general question of insurance, so far as Price
touched it, covers three questions : Life Annuities, Old-
Age Pensions, and the National Debt. We shall now
consider in turn Price's work in relation to each of these.

When *Reversionary Payments* appeared, and for some
time afterwards, the wide prevalence of unsafe societies
was a matter ' of the most serious concern '. Not in
London alone, but, to use Price's own words, ' in every
part of this kingdom there are some institutions or other
of this kind, formed just as fancy has dictated, without
any knowledge of the principles on which the values
of life-annuities and reversions ought to be calculated '.
Their formation was a ' rage ', and they were doing a
' prodigious traffic '. They were ' scenes of dishonesty on
the one hand, and of unhappy credulity on the other '.
Price termed them ' bubbles ', for the breaking of which
both justice and humanity called. He pointed out that
' the leading persons among the present members will be
the first annuitants, and they are sure of being gainers ;
and the more insufficient the scheme is on which a society
is formed the greater will be the gains of the *first* annuitants.
The same principle, therefore, that has produced and kept
up other bubbles has a tendency to preserve and promote
these.' Hence Price's fear that no argument would be
attended with any effect. He even urged that as a national
menace they should be taken ' under the notice of the

---

[1] Morgan, Introd. to 7th ed. of *Reversionary Payments*.

Legislature ', for the sufferers by them might come ' to be burdens on the public '. This was actually the case with the sufferers by the Charitable Corporation, for whose relief Parliament, in 1733, ' granted a lottery of half a million ' ; and the Company of Mercers were at the time of Price's writing ' enjoying a parliamentary aid in order to enable them to fulfil their engagements to widows ' ; while it was well known what expense was thrown on the public by the bubbles of the South Sea venture. As a matter of fact the intervention of the State was not necessary now. Price's *Reversionary Payments* did, quickly and thoroughly, what he modestly suggested nothing but State intervention could do. It created an immense sensation. On the publication of it, some of the ' societies ' dissolved at once ; some decided to reform their plans so as to make them sound ; some hesitated, while some, having effected minor improvements which were totally inadequate, still went on, only to accumulate their distress. Another event, for which Price was directly and wholly responsible, hastened the end of all ' bubble ' societies. That event was the striking success of the Equitable Society. This Society, better planned from the outset than other societies, had been offered suggestions by Price in his *Reversionary Payments*, and lost no time in seeking the further advice of the author, virtually asking him to undertake the reconstruction of its business. Price was engaged in this capacity for many years. Through his services the Society became the very first of sound Assurance Societies—' the first of its kind in the world, and increasing fast ' is the description given of it in a periodical of the time.[1] The Society had been founded in 1762. It had been refused a Charter by the Law Officers

---

[1] *Gentleman's Magazine*, vol. liii, pt. 2, p. 1039.

of the Crown on the ground that its premiums were
insufficient, ' although ', says Morgan, ' they were nearly
twice as high as they are at present ' ; [1] and it then
established itself as a voluntary association in 1765.
When Price became associated with it, it conducted its
business in modest premises near Blackfriars Bridge.
Price rode over there almost daily from Newington Green,
and his figure was well known in the streets through which
he passed. As he was seen coming on his favourite
white horse and wearing a blue great coat and black
spatter-dashers, the carmen and the orange-women could
be heard saying, ' There goes Dr. Price, make way for Dr.
Price ! ' The Equitable Society in recognition of his
invaluable services presented him with some scientific
apparatus—a telescope, a microscope, and an electrical
machine.[2] It was in connexion with his work for the
Equitable Society that he employed his nephew, William
Morgan, who, we have seen, had returned to London.
Price introduced him to the actuarial work, in which he
was destined to become an expert. Having heard of the
death of the actuary of the Society he was helping, Price,
pondering over the difficulty of finding a successor,
suddenly thought of his nephew, who was then staying
with him at Newington Green. ' Billy,' said he, ' do you
know anything of mathematics ? ' ' No, uncle,' was the
reply, ' but I can learn.' [3] Through his uncle's influence
he became assistant actuary to the Equitable Society in
February, 1774, and actuary a year later, an office which
he held for over fifty years, resigning it in December 1830.
He settled in London, his sister, Nancy Morgan, coming
up to keep house for him at Chatham Place, the house

[1] Introduction to his edition of *Reversionary Payments*.
[2] Clayden, *Early Life of Samuel Rogers*, pp. 8–9.
[3] Williams, *A Welsh Family*, p. 38.

being provided by the Society. He made a great name for himself as an actuary, and was generally known as ' Actuary Morgan '. He wrote a good deal on his subject, including a ' Review of Dr. Price's writings on the finances of Great Britain ' ; and he ' new-arranged and enlarged by the addition of algebraical and other notes and the solutions of several new problems in the doctrine of annuities' Price's *Reversionary Payments*, publishing it with an Introduction as a seventh edition.

A few years later, in 1780, Price constructed for the Equitable Society a new Table of Mortality based upon the registers of the town of Northampton. These Northampton Tables made a ' profound impression ' on ' the general mass of intelligent persons '.[1] ' Dr. Price's researches first brought to general apprehension the conviction that a large basis of observed facts is the only source of real knowledge ' [2] as to the duration and value of lives under various conditions. He raised the whole treatment of annuities to a new level, and gave to Life Insurance a scientific method. His tables were, of course, not perfect. Constructed as they were without a census, they have now been superseded. Suffice it to say that ' the Northampton Tables remained for a century by far the most important tables of mortality, employed as the basis of calculation by leading companies in Great Britain, and adopted by the Courts as practically a part of the Common Law. Parliament, followed by some State legislatures, and many courts in America, even made it the authorized standard for valuing annuity charges and reversionary interests '.[3] Price is, more than any other person, the founder of Life Insurance.

---

[1] Gow, Art. *Encycl. Brit.*, 11th ed.   [2] Ibid.

[3] Ibid.

Reversionary Payments contained schemes for the benefit of age. The ' bubble ' societies provided for old age as well as for life insurance. Price's work had precisely the same effect on their ' age ' as on their ' life ' plans. It gave to Old Age Pensions, as it gave to Life Insurance, a secure foundation. Following upon that, the provision of such pensions by the State on a contributory basis became a practical question. In 1773, a pamphlet on the subject was published by Francis Masères, Cursitor Baron of the Exchequer, ' a very able and spirited writer '. Price gave him advice and help. He was also actively associated with him in the attempt to carry into execution the design explained in it. A Bill, with suitable Tables annexed, was brought into the House of Commons. That it passed that House without much opposition is in itself eloquent testimony to the influence of Price's work. It was, however, ' rejected in the House of Lords '.[1] Another attempt was made in 1786 by the Rev. John Acland, Rector of Broad Clist. The author, in his Preface to his pamphlet,[2] describes himself as ' no Calculator, no Lawyer, no Man of Business ', but Price, who patronizes the work with a letter, dated ' Newington Green, Nov. 20, 1786 ', and with Tables and suggestions, commends the Plan it sets forth, and wishes the author ' more success than Mr. Baron Masères and myself met with some years ago '. The matter then lay dormant for some years—until 1789. In that year ' tables were computed by Dr. Price, at the request of a committee of the House of Commons, and were intended to form the foundation of a plan for enabling the labouring poor to provide support for themselves in sickness and old age, by small weekly savings from their

[1] *Reversionary Payments*, 7th ed. Edited Morgan, vol. ii, p. 473.
[2] A Plan for rendering the Poor independent on Public Contributions.

wages '. A Bill for establishing this plan, likewise, ' was
formed and approved by the Commons in the year 1789 ',
but it, too, ' was rejected by the Lords '.[1]   The non-
success of these first attempts notwithstanding, the very
fact that they were made practically and scientifically
possible by him more than by any one else, gives to Price
the distinction of being the Father of Old-Age Pensions.

However threatening to the public welfare were the
many ill-founded annuity societies, there was, in Price's
opinion, a far greater danger than they threatening it.
' These Bubbles ', says he, ' are of little consequence
compared with that Grand National Evil which is the
subject of the second chapter of this treatise.' [2] The evil
was the swelling National Debt. Every student of politics
knows how great are the evils of an exhorbitant public
debt. It was Price's view that the practice of raising the
necessary supplies for every national service by borrowing
money on interest, to be continued till the principal is
discharged must be in the highest degree detrimental,
unless, that is, there exist means of paying off the debts
regularly.   As he put it, ' mortgaging posterity and
funding for eternity ' in order to pay interest ' must in
the end prove destructive '. Price regarded the National
Debt as a political as well as an economic evil : it tended
alarmingly to increase subserviency to the Crown, and so
was a serious menace to liberty. The increase in the debt
had been great. At the opening of the century the debt was
sixteen millions ; before the third quarter of the century
had ended it stood at 138 millions. At this rate, thought
Price, ' no resources can be sufficient to support a kingdom
long '. One way of escape, he pointed out, would be to

[1] A Plan for rendering the Poor independent on Public Contributions.   [2] *Reversionary Payments*, 3rd ed., Preface.

borrow no money except on annuities which were to terminate within a given period. This would, it is true, increase
the *present* burden of the State, but it would set a limit
beyond which the debt could not increase. He did not
recommend this plan, however. It may be worth
pointing out that Price was in favour of a tax on bachelors,
and was of opinion that the revenue derived from it would
suffice to clear the debt. ' One of the properest objects of
taxation in a State is Celibacy ', said he. ' I doubt not
but that by a fund supplied from hence the end I have in
view might have been easily accomplished.' He did no
more than thus briefly mention this plan. The plan
he recommended was the provision of ' an annual saving,
to be applied invariably, together with the interest of all
the sums redeemed by it, to the purpose of discharging
the public debts ', or, in other words, ' the establishment
of a permanent Sinking Fund '.[1] A Sinking Fund had been
established in 1716, but it did not begin its operation until
1719. The practice of alienating it was begun in 1733,
and continued, with the result that its efficacy was
practically destroyed. Price's proposal, really, was for
its *re*-establishment. The great advantage, in Price's
mind, of such a Fund was its increasing itself by compound
interest. The smallest Fund of this kind ' is, indeed,
omnipotent, if it is allowed time to operate. He offered
a simple but arresting example : ' A *penny*, so improved
from our Saviour's birth, as to double itself every fourteen
years, or, which is nearly the same, put out to five per cent.
compound interest at our Saviour's birth, would, by this
time [1771], have increased to more money than would
be contained in 150 millions of globes, each equal to the
earth in magnitude, and all solid gold. A *shilling*, put

[1] Ibid., p. 137.

out to six per cent. compound interest, would, in the
same time, have increased to a greater sum in gold than
the whole solar system could hold, supposing it a sphere
equal in diameter to the diameter of Saturn's orbit. And
the earth is to such a sphere nearly as half a square foot,
or a quarto page, to the whole surface of the earth.' [1] Such
was the power of compound interest, Price's great specific.
His only fear was that ' we are got so near to the limits
of the resources of the nation ' that the Fund ' cannot be
allowed much time ' ; and to make up for this it would
necessarily have to be large. He was so apprehensive of
the future financial prospects of the kingdom that he
firmly believed that unless such a fund would be established there was nothing to do but ' wait the issue, and
tremble ', for ' the consequences must be fatal '. It was
that apprehension and the conviction that he would be
doing the little in his power to avert the calamity,
that made him publish his thoughts more fully on the
subject. They appeared under the title, *An Appeal to the
Public on the Subject of the National Debt*. The work
was well received, and Lord North spoke highly of it in
Parliament.

It was Price's interest in national finance that gave rise
to his friendship with Turgot, the eminent French statesman and economist, and Necker, the Genevese Director-
General of Finances in France. Through them, Price's
writings had definite influence on the financial arrangements of the French Government. Some years later,
Shelburne was able to write to his friend, ' I take it for
granted that you have seen the edict, just now published
in France, adopting your principles into their finance, as
far as comes within the power of their government without

---

[1] *Reversionary Payments*, Preface to 1st ed.

overturning the principles of it. If you have not, I can send it to you '.[1]

It is in the same Treatise that Price discusses the population of this country. The question was a much discussed one at the time. The conflicting views were based, of course, on indirect evidence, there being no census. Price's view was a gloomy one. He thought that the country was becoming depopulated, some of the reasons he adduced for the depopulation being the neglect of agriculture, the prevalence of luxury, and the growth of large towns. His view, it is hardly necessary to point out, was an erroneous one.

The year of the publication of *Reversionary Payments*, and those immediately following, found Price earnestly employed in struggles for religious liberty in matters affecting not Dissenters only but members of the Established Church as well. The Dissenters, however, were very actively interested, and Price's talents and virtues placed him at their head. He was among the foremost to urge upon the public the need for reform, and he always expressed himself in warm and eloquent language. His strenuous zeal, so manifest at public meetings, greatly encouraged the people in their resolution to attempt reform. During 1771–2 some clergy and laity of the Established Church inaugurated a movement for relief from subscription to the Thirty-nine Articles. Early in the latter year they appealed to Parliament, but unsuccessfully. At the debate in the House, two Dissenting ministers were present, Edward Pickard, of Carter Lane, and Dr. Philip Furneaux, of Chatham. These two, receiving the active co-operation of Price, conferred with

---

[1] ' Bowood Park, 7 Oct. 1784 '. In *Letters to and from Richard Price*, Mass. Hist. Soc. In further references these letters will be referred to as the *Price Letters*.

others of their brethren after the debate, and at once
summoned to a general meeting of ministers the representative ministers of the three great denominations,
Presbyterians, Independents, and Baptists, in and near
London, who constituted the ' Dissenting Deputies '—
a body founded in 1732 to prosecute the agitation for
religious freedom.   The meeting agreed to make an
application to Parliament for relief from subscription.
Price was elected a member of the Committee which was
entrusted with preparing and conducting the application.[1]
The Press contained numerous letters for and against
relief ; addresses to, and from, clergymen of all ranks,
including the Archbishop of Canterbury, appeared, and
pamphlets were published both anonymously and under
the names of eminent men.   The application to Parliament
was made in 1772.   The Bill for relief passed the Commons twice—in an amended form in 1773—but was twice
rejected by the Lords.   The debate was notable for
a speech in favour of the Bill by the great Chatham, who
was on very friendly terms with Price.   In reply to
the Archbishop of York's description of Dissenters as
' men of close ambition ', he said that ' that was judging
uncharitably ', and, after a pause, continued, ' The Dissenting Ministers are represented as men of close ambition.
They are so my lords ; and their ambition is to keep close
to the college of fishermen, not of cardinals, and to the
doctrine of inspired apostles, not to the decrees of interested
and aspiring bishops.   They contend for a spiritual creed
and a scriptural worship.'   Referring to the Established
Church, he added in a now famous witticism, ' We have
a Calvinistic creed, a Popish liturgy, and an Arminian
Clergy '.   Soon after the debate Chatham wrote to Price

---

[1] Turner, *Lives of Eminent Unitarians*, vol. ii, p. 409.

from Burton Pynsent on January 16, 1773, a letter in
which he pays a neat compliment to Price's great
work in the cause of religious liberty. ' In writing
to you,' he says, ' it is impossible the mind should not go
of itself to that most interesting of all objects to fallible
man—Toleration.' He assures Price that ' on this sacred
and inalienable right of nature, and bulwark of truth ', his
' warm wishes will always keep pace ' with his. ' Happy ',
adds he, ' if the times had allowed us to add hopes to our
wishes.' [1] Complete relief was not obtained, but in a few
years a Bill was passed by both Houses exchanging
subscription for a simple declaration of Christianity,
Protestantism, and acceptance of the Scriptures. Price,
however, while appreciating the advance thus made, found
in the modified requirement a fundamental objection ; it
was still an imposition by the state. He, therefore, was one
of a small minority who were for refusing its acceptance
on the ground that though the requirement was ' one
which they could conscientiously subscribe ', it was
objectionable ' as implying an acknowledgement of what
they denied *in toto*, that the civil magistrate had a right
to interfere at all in matters of conscience '.[2]

Late in the sixties of the century Priestley conceived
and executed his plan for publishing a periodical whose
pages would be open for the expression of all views of
Christianity, including those opposed to it, but the
articles were all expected to be original contributions.
Among those who promised their assistance was Dr.
Kippis ; and one of the names lent as patrons was that
of ' Richard Price '. This publication, the *Theological
Repository*, may be regarded as the earliest Unitarian

---

[1] Price, *Love of Our Country*, p. 38 n.
[2] Turner, *Lives of Eminent Unitarians*, vol. ii, p. 409.

periodical. Price, though a patron, contributed no articles to it.[1]

During the early seventies, a movement was in progress to establish a Unitarian Chapel in London. Theophilus Lindsey was the moving spirit. He was supported by Price, the Arian, and Priestley, the Socinian, who were ' active and zealous friends ' of the movement. They offered by subscription of their friends to indemnify Lindsey on his first venture, which made the project possible. Accordingly the first Unitarian Chapel was opened by Lindsey on Sunday, April 17, 1774.[2] ' Unitarianism ' was a term of much less definite connotation than either ' Arianism ' or ' Socinianism '. It was at times and by various writers, opposed to each, whereas by other writers it was used as including both, since they were alike anti-Trinitarian. The Unitarianism of Lindsey, however, was Socinianism, which was more remote from orthodoxy than Arianism. Price remained an Arian all his life, but his was ' low ' Arianism, a form nearer to Socinianism than to orthodoxy.[3]

During these years, Price's congregations were increasing greatly, owing, no doubt, to his rapidly growing fame and popularity. In spite of busy days, he gave of his best to the pulpit. Nor did he neglect the pastoral side of his ministry, for he would manage to devote some portion of most afternoons, and all of some afternoons, to visiting his flock. The calls upon his time from sources outside his congregations were becoming exceedingly numerous, and his circle of friends was becoming a very wide one. Some evenings each week he spent in atten-

[1] See McLachlan, *The Story of a Nonconformist Library*, pp. 88–104.

[2] Belsham, *Memoirs of Theophilus Lindsey*, pp. 72–4.

[3] See p. 115 ff., *infra*.

dance at parties. The clubs or parties meeting in London in the eighteenth century were a remarkable institution. Their members discussed almost everything that human knowledge embraced, and the discussions were on a high plane. The best and ablest men of the time attended them, some being members of more than one such circle. Price was a member of two. He attended one which used to meet on Friday evenings in the house of its members, amongst whom were his neighbour, Thomas Rogers, and two celebrated literary women, Mrs. Elizabeth Montague, one of the best-known of the 'blue-stockings', and Mrs. Hester Chapone, an essayist of ability and taste. But his favourite party was that which met, first in a Coffee-house in St. Paul's Churchyard, and later in the London Coffee-house, Ludgate-hill. Among its members were Benjamin Franklin, while he was in England, John Canton, Dr. Andrew Kippis, and Dr. Joseph Priestley. In this company, discussing science, philosophy, and theology, Price was 'most agreeably entertained'. He induced Shelburne to offer Priestley the post of Librarian, at a very liberal salary, with residence at Calne in winter, and in London in summer, and a pension upon his ceasing to hold the office. The opportunities which Priestley thus obtained had much influence on his development.

CHAPTER V

American War of Independence — opinion in England — Price in touch with the Colonists — Thomas Paine's *Common Sense* — Price's *Observations on the Nature of Civil Liberty* — enormous sale — translated on the Continent and reprinted in America — replies to it by Burke, Johnson, Wesley, and others — Freedom of the City of London — America declares her Independence — Plan in *Civil Liberty* to secure permanent peace — Price the prophet of the League of Nations — The Constitution of America — Price again in touch with France — Welshmen at the foundation of the American Republic.

PRICE now stood on the threshold of the struggle between the American colonies and Britain which ended in the proclamation of their Independence by the colonies. The history of the struggle need not be given here ; every reader knows it in sufficient outline. The essence of the quarrel is expressed by the well-known maxim, 'No taxation without representation'. Price anxiously watched the struggle from its very commencement.

Opinion in England was by no means wholly on the side of the Government. In the Whig Party, Burke, Chatham, and others advocated reconciliation. Among these others were John Dunning, afterwards Lord Ashburton, one of the greatest lawyers of the century, and of whom John Lee, who himself became a Solicitor-General, said that, ' his abilities are unequalled by any man's I ever knew ',[1] and Colonel Isaac Barré, of ' Sons of Liberty ' fame. Both were not only friends but warm admirers of Price. The protest of the City of London against the Government

[1] Letter to a friend in the Country, Jan. 31, 1772.

policy represented a large volume of opinion outside Parliament. Several little incidents were significant. On hearing of the battle of Lexington,[1] Thomas Rogers, Price's neighbour, and father of the poet, put on mourning. Being asked if he had lost a friend, he answered that he had lost several friends—in New England.[2] The Recorder of London ' put on mourning for the same event at the same time ', and Grenville Sharp ' gave up his place in the Ordnance Office because he did not think it right to ship stores and munitions of war which might be used to put down self-government in the American colonies '.[3] Chatham ' withdrew his eldest son from the army rather than suffer him to be engaged in the war '.[4] Lord Effingham ' for the same reason threw up his commission '.[5] Amherst ' is said to have refused the command against the Americans '.[6] The main body of opposition to the war lay in the Dissenting Churches and in the large trading towns. On the other hand, the landed gentry, the Established Church, the army, and the ' stress of legal opinion ' were for the war and against the Americans.[7] It was these last that on the whole represented the prevailing view in the country. It is all-important to notice that it was not independence, but reconciliation, that the supporters of America desired ; and it was all that the Americans themselves desired also. The idea of independence was not what inspired the Americans in their struggle, at least up to the actual outbreak of war.[8]

[1] The outbreak of the war, April 19, 1775.

[2] Clayden, *Early Life of Samuel Rogers*, p. 33.

[3] Ibid.

[4] Lecky, *History of England in the Eighteenth Century*, vol. iii, p. 532.

[5] Ibid.   [6] Ibid.   [7] Ibid., pp. 529–30.

[8] Bancroft, *History of the United States*, vol. vii, p. 188.

Franklin told Chatham that he ' never heard from any
person the least expression of a wish for separation '.
Washington said that ' no such thing as independence is
desired by any thinking man in America '. Jefferson
declared that ' before the 19th of April, 1775, I never
heard a whisper of disposition to separate from Great
Britain '.[1] It was after the outbreak of war that independence was thought of, and even then reconciliation
was not completely abandoned. Indeed, it seems that it
was Turgot, the French economist, who was ' the first to
foretell and to desire ' independence. The idea, however,
soon found advocates in England. Josiah Tucker, a
Carmarthenshire Welshman who had become Dean of
Gloucester, and a political economist of distinct Royalist
tendencies, ' sought to convince the landed gentry that
Great Britain would lose nothing if she should renounce
her colonies and cultivate commerce with them as an
independent nation ',[2] and persons in high position
praised him for it. John Millar, the Professor of Law in
the University of Glasgow, taught the youth of Scotland
who attended his lectures that ' the republican form of
government is by far the best, either for a very small
or a very extensive country '.[3] A greater and more
renowned Scotsman still, Adam Smith, of *Wealth of
Nations* fame, the teacher of statesmen, would have
the colonies ' either fairly represented in Parliament or
independent '.[4] It was not long before there became quite
prevalent in this country the view, based on the concrete
situation, that independence would soon be achieved by
the struggling Americans. Shelburne, in Oct. 1775, was
expressing the opinion of those who were competent to

---

[1] Bancroft, *History of the United States*, vol. vii, p, 188.
[2] Ibid., p. 103.   [3] Ibid., pp. 101–2.   [4] Ibid.

judge, when he wrote to Price, ' I look upon the colonies as lost '.[1]

Price had been in close touch with the colonists for a considerable time. His nephew, George Cadogan Morgan, while at his uncle's house on the Green, met many of the most conspicuous of those who sympathized with America, and some foremost Americans. Price regarded the struggle as vitally important both to this country and to America. It was a struggle, and a ' last ' struggle, for the ' sacred blessing of liberty '. His heart burned with fiery zeal for liberty, and eloquently did he urge the colonists to defend it. ' For my own part,' says he, ' were I in America I would go barefoot ; I would cover myself with skins and endure any inconvenience sooner than give up the vast stake now depending ; and I should be encouraged in this by knowing that my difficulties would be temporary, and that I was engaged in a last struggle for liberty, which perseverance would certainly crown with success.' He spoke with earnestness because he was thoroughly convinced that the authority claimed by this country over the colonies was ' a despotism which would leave them none of the rights of freemen '. ' I consider America ', he continues, ' as an asylum for the friends of liberty here, which it would be a dreadful calamity to lose.' [2] The same letter further emphasizes the significance he attached to the struggle : ' By the government which our ministers *endeavour* to establish in New England, and that which they *have* established in Canada, we see what sort of government they *wish for* in this country ; and as far as they can succeed in America, their way will be paved for success here. Indeed, the

---

[1] *Price Letters.*
[2] Ibid., Letter to Richard Chauncey ; ' Newington, Feb. 25, 1775.'

influence of the crown has already in effect subverted
liberty here ; and should this influence be able to
establish itself in America, and gain an accession of
strength from thence, our fate would be sealed, and
all security for the sacred blessing of liberty would be
destroyed in every part of the British dominions. These
are sentiments which dwell much upon my heart and
I am often repeating them.'   With his usual magnanimity
he says, ' Forgive your oppressors ; I believe they know
not what they do ' ; and with a determination to follow
the right that is perfectly consonant with a most charitable
nature, he adds, ' but at the same time make them know
that you *will* be free '.   ' God ', he confidently and en-
couragingly reminds the colonists, ' is on the side of
liberty and justice.'   It is said that ' it was Dr. Price's pen
that advised the City of Boston to throw the taxed tea
into the sea ', in 1773.[1] Foreseeing, in April 1775, that the
struggle was inevitably developing into an armed conflict,
he expressed the hope that the colonists would show ' that
they deserve to be *free* by showing themselves *brave* '.[2]
So much were Price's opinions valued and such was the
confidence placed in them by the colonists that one of his
correspondents informed him that he thought fit to
publish, ' with the proper precautions ', some extracts
from Price's letter to him.   ' I should think myself
wanting in my duty to my countrymen ', he tells Price,
' if I should confine within the narrow circle of my
particular acquaintance, what is so excellently fitted to
direct them in the true line of conduct they ought to
pursue.'[3]   In a few weeks after the commencement of
hostilities all direct communication between Britain and

---

[1] Williams, *A Welsh Family*, p. 41.

[2] In *Price Letters* : Letter to Josiah Quincey.

[3] Ibid., John Winthrop to Price.

the colonies was cut off. Price was, however, still receiving, and, as yet, sending, news. He managed it through his friend Franklin, who was the ambassador of the colonies in Paris. This indirect communication was kept up for a considerable time during the period when reliable news about the progress of the struggle was difficult to obtain in England. Price, therefore, was in a specially advantageous position to know at first hand how affairs were proceeding.

The war had been going on for six months, and the situation was quickly developing into what Shelburne, without exaggeration, described as ' a dreadful crisis '. It was at this point that Price, who had already, at the very beginning of the war, written against its injustice under the signature of ' Aurelius ' in the *Gazette*, and who had since watched the course of events with informed judgement if with sympathetic anxiety, decided to take his full part in the struggle.

Thomas Paine, then living in America, wrote his pamphlet *Common Sense* to further the cause of American Independence. He published it in America in January, 1776, and it made a tremendous impression.[1] But the work which stands out as of paramount importance in influencing public opinion in this country, and which at the same time had immense influence in America as well, was one entitled *Observations on the Nature of Civil Liberty, the Principles of Government, and the Justice and Policy of the War with America*, by Richard Price. The work, which, the author tells us in the Preface, contained ' the sentiments of a private and unconnected man ', was a philosophic examination of the foundations of the American problem. It was prepared in the winter of 1775–6, and

---

[1] Conway, *Life of Thomas Paine*, p. 25.

published in February 1776, at the price of two shillings.
Thus the two works which stand alone in their importance
in relation to the American cause were prepared and
published, the one in America, and the other in Britain,
almost coincidently.   Price's work was not only favour-
ably, but eagerly, received by the public.   It was an
eloquent defence of liberty and of America's struggle
therefor ; it had a powerful added interest in its focussing
of attention upon the imperfect liberty enjoyed in England,
owing to defects in the latter's representation.   The
pamphlet was a clever adaptation of the case of America
to conditions at home.   So universally was it sought that
' the press could not supply the demand for it '.[1]   Several
thousand copies were sold in the course of a few days.
It ran into five editions in as many weeks,[2] and into over
a dozen editions in the course of the year.   The friends of
America thought they could not better serve their cause
than by extending the sale of it to all ranks of society.
Application was therefore made to Price for permission to
print a cheap edition of it.   With a noble disinterestedness
he granted this without hesitation, publishing an edition
at the price of sixpence, sacrificing, in so doing, private
profits which would have been very considerable.   Private
profit, however, was the last thing he was thinking of.
The work now reached all classes of people—even the
very lowest.   Over 60,000 copies of it—an enormous
number for those days—were sold in the course of the
year of its publication.   Price's name was immediately
on everybody's lips.   People in the highest station were
eagerly curious and interested to know him.   ' When
Dr. Price ', says Rogers, ' was standing one day in the

---

[1] Morgan, *Memoirs*, p. 58.

[2] The Preface to the 1st edition is dated ' Feb. 8, 1776 ' ; that to
5th edition, ' March 16, 1776 '.

gallery of the House of Commons, a rumour ran through the crowd that he was there, and a gentleman who sat near him asked him very impatiently which was Dr. Price, and he often laughed at his own embarrassment.'[1] Hardly was *Civil Liberty* published than it aroused a storm of replies. One of these was by Edmund Burke in his *Letter to the Sheriffs of Bristol*. Burke had urged conciliation with the colonies, but he had never denied the right of the British Parliament to tax them. The Whig Party, to which he belonged, had several sections. Burke, as a member of the Rockinghamite section, never departed from the principle, so obnoxious to the colonies, which was laid down in Rockingham's Declaratory Act— declaring the right of the British Parliament to legislate for the colonies ' in all cases whatsoever '—an Act of which Price said, ' I defy any one to define slavery in stronger terms '. All along Burke had opposed the war, not on the ground of principle, but on the ground of expediency. For the Government a host of writers appeared, many of them, among whom was Dr. Johnson, being the ' immediate pensioners of the Government '. Dr. Markham, Archbishop of York, Dr. Lowth, Bishop of London, and the renowned John Wesley, all replied to Price. The reply of one of the Government's pensioned writers, Dr. Shebbeare, exemplifies the character of much of what was written by others. Shebbeare was a notorious libeller. He had even been placed in the pillory for libel on former occasions. His pamphlet breathed nothing but coarse invective and abuse ; and scurrilous writings by him against Price are to be found in many of the papers for the year 1776. Perhaps the most popular of all the replies to Price was that by Goodricke in a pamphlet entitled *Observations on*

---

[1] Williams, *A Welsh Family*, p. 42.

Dr. Price's Theory and Principles of Civil Liberty and Government. Price made no formal reply to any of these ; though other writers did. All Price did was to take passing notice of some points in another publication in the following year. The arguments of the best of his opponents did not, in his opinion, require a reply beyond the very brief word he gave to them in his Introduction to another pamphlet in the following year ; [1] and the abuse of a great number of them neither disturbed his repose nor excited his resentment. In spite of all arguments and abuse, the *Observations on Civil Liberty* held the field as by far the most important work on the American question published in this country. It was translated into several languages and circulated extensively on the Continent, especially in Holland and Germany. As early as March 14, 1776, that is, a little more than a month after its publication, the work brought Price the thanks of the Council of the City of London for his having laid down in it ' those pure principles upon which alone the supreme legislative authority of Great Britain over her colonies can be justly or beneficially maintained ', and his having held forth ' those public objects without which it must be totally indifferent to the kingdom who are in, or who are out of, power '. The Council further conferred upon him the highest honour it had in its power to confer—the Freedom of the City. This was extended to him ' in a gold box of the value of £50 ' as a ' graceful testimony ' of approval of the *Observations*.[2] On March 23, Price sent from Newington Green to ' Wm. Rix, Esq., Town-Clerk ' his ' warmest acknowledgements ', saying that the *Observations* were written ' with no other intention than

---

[1] See pp. 83–4 infra.
[2] London's Roll of Fame, at the Guildhall Library.

to plead the cause of liberty and justice, and to remind this country of the dreadful danger of its present situation ', and expressing the hope that ' the testimony of approbation which they have received from a body so respectable, annually elected by the first City in the world, and so distinguished for giving an example of zeal in the cause of liberty ', would ' lead the public to fix their views more on such measures as shall save a sinking Constitution and preserve us from impending calamities '.[1] On July 21, after receiving the Freedom at the hands of the Chamberlain, he conveyed again from Newington Green his thanks for ' the great honour '. ' May the City of London always flourish ', he exclaims ; and ' may the kingdom be delivered from the dreadful danger with which it is threatened by the present Civil War '.[2] There is a good story of the meeting, soon after the publication of the *Observations*, of the Duke of Cumberland, brother of the king, Lord Ashburton, the great lawyer, and Price. They were at the Bar of the House of Lords when the Duke told Price that ' he had read his Essay on Civil Liberty till he was blind '. ' It is remarkable ', replied Ashburton, ' that your royal highness should have been blinded by a book which has opened the eyes of all mankind.' [3]

Civil Liberty soon found its way across the Atlantic, and circulated throughout the length and breadth of America. It was reprinted at Boston, New York, and Philadelphia. In England, its effect was to transform a large volume of public opinion and create an atmosphere more favourable to the colonists. Though the creation of that atmosphere was not necessary in America, its effect was none the less substantial there. With Paine's

---

[1] London's Roll of Fame.   [2] Ibid.
[3] Clayden, *Early Life of Samuel Rogers*, p. 33.

Common Sense, which had been circulated a short time before it, Richard Price's *Observations on Civil Liberty* was a powerful, and it may well be the decisive, factor in the determination of America to declare its Independence. This it did on July 4, 1776—less than five months after the first appearance of the work. The drawing up of the Declaration had been entrusted to Thomas Jefferson, Benjamin Franklin, and two others. His three colleagues asked Jefferson to make a first draft of it. This was so well done that it was accepted without any changes other than a few verbal ones. Its opening paragraphs strike the note of the whole and give it a philosophical foundation :
' We hold these truths to be self-evident, that all men are created equal, that they are endowed by their Creator with certain inalienable Rights, that among these are Life, Liberty, and the pursuit of Happiness. That to secure these Rights Governments are instituted among Men, deriving their just powers from the consent of the Governed, that whenever any Form of Government becomes destructive of these ends, it is the Right of the People to alter or to abolish it, and to institute new Government, laying its foundation on such principles and organizing its powers in such form as to them shall seem most likely to effect their Safety and Happiness.' Here we have clearly stated the *a priori* doctrines of Equality, Natural Rights, and Sovereignty of the People. To this philosophy, Price's *Civil Liberty* had given bold expression. Broadly, Price's work follows the political philosophy of Locke, and adopts the ' contract ' theory of government. We may take a brief glance at the work itself. It consists of two parts, the first examining the idea of Civil Liberty, and the second, the justice of the War. The second has much less value to-day than the first, whose philosophy, closely and logically argued, has permanent value. It is

the spirit and temper which pervade this work which have made and inspired modern democracy. Particularly, too, both its prophetic insistence upon the need of a League of Nations, and the brilliant success, in the Constitution of the United States, of a scheme of administration such as it outlines, give it abiding interest and worth.

Price views Liberty as physical, moral, religious, and civil. Its essential feature, the feature which is common to all its forms, is self-direction or self-government. This is the dividing line between Liberty and Slavery, and ' as far as any cause comes in to restrain the power of self-government, so far slavery is introduced '. Civil Liberty is ' the power of a Civil Society or State to govern itself by its own discretion, or by laws of its own making, without being subject to any foreign direction, or to the impositions of any extraneous will or power '.[1] Consistently with this, ' all civil government, so far as it can be denominated free, is the creature of the people '.[2] And in every free state, therefore, ' every man is his own legislator ; all taxes are free gifts for public services ; all laws are particular provisions or regulations established by common consent for gaining protection and safety ; and all magistrates are trustees or Deputies for carrying these regulations into execution '.[3] Price here gives a more concise, logical, and succinct expression to the spirit of free government than either Locke or Rousseau, both of whom had greatly influenced thought, and Price's thought particularly, in this direction.

The consideration of the best means to prevent war leads Price to a suggestion of the utmost importance,

---

[1] *Civil Liberty*, p. 3. [2] Ibid., p. 6.
[3] Ibid., p. 3.

and which distinctly makes him the prophet of the League
of Nations. He sees that the division of Europe into a
great number of independent kingdoms with continually
clashing interests is bound to be a frequent cause of war.
It would be no remedy, he urges, to make one of these
states supreme over the rest, for that would be ' to subject
all the states to the arbitrary direction of one, and to
establish an ignominious slavery not possible to be long
endured '. That could not be approved by any mind
that has not lost every idea of Civil Liberty. On the
contrary, says Price, seizing directly the idea of a League
of Nations : ' Let every state with respect to all its
internal concerns, be continued independent of all the
rest ; and let a general confederacy be formed by the
appointment of a Senate consisting of Representatives
from all the different states. Let this Senate possess the
power of managing all the *common* concerns of the united
states, and of judging and deciding between them, as
a common *Arbiter* or *Umpire*, in all disputes ; having at
the same time, under its direction, the common force of
the states to support its decisions.—In these circumstances,
each separate state would be secure against the inter-
ference of foreign power in its private concerns, and,
therefore, would possess Liberty ; and at the same time
it would be secure against all oppression and insult from
every neighbouring state.—Thus might the scattered force
and abilities of a whole continent be gathered into one
point ; all litigations settled as they rose ; universal peace
preserved ; and nation prevented from any more lifting
up sword against nation.' [1] Here is a clear vision of the
ideal which fiery experiences have revealed, though not
a whit more clearly, to the world of our day. Here, too,

---

[1] *Civil Liberty*, pp. 8–9.

is the first expression of the ideal in the English language. It is not quite the first appearance of the idea in the whole history of thought : in expressing it Price ' followed Leibnitz, as he anticipated Kant '.[1] Moreover, it is noteworthy that the constitution of the United States of America, formed very soon after the publication of *Civil Liberty*, is fundamentally on the lines of this plan, and that the plan, therefore, we must believe, cannot but have at least confirmed, if, indeed, it did not lead, the judgement of those who framed that conspicuously successful constitution of ' united states ' autonomous in certain respects and subject to a central authority in others.   The advocacy of a confederacy or League of Nations by America in our day reminds us that that great country's voice echoes a voice whose utterance in the cause of Liberty, and of America itself, gave expression to the ideal nearly a hundred and fifty years before.

Price's *Civil Liberty* brought him again the famous Frenchmen, Turgot, Necker, and Condorcet, as correspondents.   Through them, therefore, Price's ideas must have gained added popularity with thinking men in France.   The fact should be borne in mind in view of the extremely important part played by ' philosophy ' in bringing about the upheaval in that country at the close of the next decade.

In view of the fact that Price was a Welshman, it is worth our noting how prominent a part was played by Welshmen in the establishment of what has become the leading Republic in the world.[2]   Thomas Jefferson, who drew up the Declaration, was Welsh, his ancestors having migrated to America from the Snowdon district.   Of those

[1] Brailsford, *Shelley, Godwin, and their Circle*, H. U. L., p. 11.

[2] Most of the facts here given are drawn from an Article by Dr. Joseph Roberts, New York, in *Y Traethodydd*, for 1900.

who signed that historic document many were the
descendants of Welsh immigrants, while some were them-
selves born in Wales. Such were : John Adams, Samuel
Adams, Button Gwinnett, Benjamin Harrison, Stephen
Hopkins, Francis Hopkinson, Richard Henry Lee, Francis
Henry Lightfoot Lee, Francis Lewis, William Lloyd,
Arthur Middleton, Lewis Morris, Robert Morris, John
Morton, John Penn, and William Williams. John Adams
and Thomas Jefferson became in succession after George
Washington Presidents of the Republic. Francis Hopkin-
son was the author of ' Hail Columbia ', one of America's
National Songs. The American Army had a number of
Welshmen in high command. They included fourteen
Generals : John Cadwaladr, William Davies, Andrew
Lewis, Morgan Lewis, Charles Lee, Daniel Morgan, James
Rees, Isaac Shelby, Edward Stephens, John Thomas,
Anthony Wayne, Joseph Williams, Otto Williams, and
Richard Winn. Of these, Anthony Wayne was almost as
famous in his day as Washington ; and Charles Lee, who
was for a considerable period second in command, was
recognized as one of the ablest Generals in the Army, and
was a great linguist. He was buried in the same cemetery
as Benjamin Franklin, in Philadelphia. In addition, we
find a Welshman in the person of Dr. John Morgan filling
the post of Chief Surgeon of the Army ; while another,
Robert Morris, is said to have borne the greatest part of
the burden of financing the Army out of his own private
means.

CHAPTER VI

In the Spring of the following year, 1777, probably at the end of March,[1] Price published another pamphlet entitled *Additional Observations on the Nature and Value of Civil Liberty and the War with America*, and dedicated it ' To the Right Honourable the Lord Mayor, the Aldermen and the Commons of the City of London '. These *Additional Observations*, which their author describes as ' supplemental and explanatory ', are another treatise on the lines of the former. With events promising ' a tragical and deplorable issue ', he humbly acquits himself in the Introduction with the words, ' I shall always reflect with satisfaction, that I have, though a private person of little consequence, borne my testimony from deep-felt conviction, against a war which must shock the feelings and reason of every considerate person '. He has ' avoided entering into any controversy with the crowd of writers who have published remarks ' on the former pamphlet ;

---

[1] See Doran, *Last Journals of Horace Walpole*, vol. ii, p. 16.

but being ' unwilling to overlook them entirely ' he refers
to them briefly and ' once for all ', in the Introduction.
He thanks those friends, ' all unknown ' to him, who have
vindicated him, and assures them that though he has
been silent he has not been ' inattentive to their arguments
nor insensible of their candour '. He tenders his acknowledgements to those who have opposed him ' without
abuse or rancour ', amongst whom he ranks Goodricke,
Hey, Fletcher, and Wesley ; [1] and mentions that there
may be others though they have not happened to fall into
his hands. The replies of these writers contain ' all of
most importance which has been urged against me in the
way of argument ', and Price contents himself with leaving
' every one who has read them or shall read them to
decide for himself how far they have succeeded '. Lastly,
he acknowledges himself ' indebted ' to those writers,
' who, under the name of Answers, have published violent
invectives ' against him, for they have forgotten that
' abuse and scurrility always defeat their own ends, and
hurt the cause they are employed to serve '. He refrains
from any attempt at giving a list of them—' they are
without number '. He refers to one only, whom he
considers the ablest. This writer, who published anonymously, was Mr. John Lind, but Price, though no doubt
he knew his identity, refers to him as ' the author of the
Three Letters to Dr. Price '. He was a barrister, better
known as a contributor to the newspapers under the
signature of ' Attilius ', and as the supposed author of
the ' Answer to the Declaration of Independence '. Price
dismisses his notion, which was also Wesley's notion,
that civil governors are omnipotent, and that there can

---

[1] See ' List of Works occasioned by Price ', at the end of this
volume.

therefore be no liberty against them, with the remark, ' Charming doctrine this for Russia and Turkey '. Price means his *Additional Observations* to be his last intrusion into political affairs. ' I now leave an open field ', says he as he closes the Introduction, ' to all who shall please to take any further notice of me. Wishing them the same satisfaction that I have felt in *meaning* to promote peace and justice, and looking higher than this world of strife and tumult—I withdraw from politics.' Elsewhere, too, and within a very few months of his writing these words, he expresses the same intention. ' I have taken my leave of politics ', he tells one of his American friends, ' and am now in the situation of a silent spectator waiting with inexpressible anxiety the issue of one of the most important struggles that ever took place among mankind '.[1] The virulence of replies was only a part of what he had to suffer. Anonymous letters, which he carefully concealed from his wife, were sent threatening his life. It was in the house of his neighbour, Thomas Rogers, that much of his correspondence was received and kept. Handbills were circulated stating that he was in league with the enemy. In the letter to Winthrop just quoted he says ' I am become a person so marked and obnoxious that prudence requires me to be very cautious '. So true was this, he bewails, that he had to ' avoid all correspondence ' with Dr. Franklin, who was then in Paris.

The *Additional Observations* sold rapidly. Like its predecessor this work, too, reached the Continent and was reprinted in America. Baron Van der Capellan, a very eminent Dutch statesman of those times, who translated both pamphlets, wrote to Price after receiving

[1] In *Price Letters* : To John Winthrop, dated ' London, June 15, 1777 '.

this second pamphlet complimenting him upon his having
' deserved so well ' not only from his country, but ' from
mankind in general '.[1] And Arthur Lee sent from
America the testimony ' I never in my life read anything
with more satisfaction '.[2]

The *Additional Observations* is divided into three parts,
the second and third of which deal with financial matters
and are almost wholly statistical. The first part, as in
the case of the former *Observations*, is a philosophical
analysis of Civil Liberty, and is, like it, of permanent
value. The line of argument is also the same, but with
important amplifications on several points.

In 1778, the *Observations* and the *Additional Observations*
were issued together, with a General Introduction, under
the title, *Two Tracts on Civil Liberty*. In the same year
Price tells Priestley that in spite of all abuses and suspicion,
he reckons the publication of his work on Civil Liberty
' one of the best actions of my life '.[3] Nowhere, however,
were Price's interest in, and his services to, the American
cause more appreciated than in America itself. After
declaring their Independence, in 1776, the colonists at
once set about stabilizing their financial position, and it
was to Price that they again turned. He had made a
name for himself as a financier before he wrote on Civil
Liberty, and both his tracts on that subject contained
reviews of state finance. Now there came to him an
outstanding tribute to his ability and authority in this
capacity. On October 6, 1778, the American Congress
resolved, ' That the Honourable Benjamin Franklin,
Arthur Lee, and John Adams, Esquires, or any one of
them, be directed forthwith to apply to Dr. Price and

Clayden, *Early Life of Samuel Rogers*, p. 34.
[2] ' Dec. 14, 1777 '. In *Price Letters*.
[3] ' April 20, 1777 '. Ibid.

inform him that it is the desire of Congress to consider him as a Citizen of the United States, and to receive his assistance in regulating their finances. That if he shall think it expedient to remove with his family to America and afford such assistance, a generous provision shall be made for requiting his services.' [1] The three persons named have ' much satisfaction in communicating ' this resolution ' from a great respect to the character of Dr. Price '. ' You may depend on us ', they tell him, ' to discharge the expense of your journey and voyage and for every assistance in our power to make your passage agreeable, as well as your reception and accommodation in our country.' Lee wrote him a letter on the 8th of the following December pointing out the extent to which ' the future happiness of a people depends on the proper management of their finances '. His entreaty to Price is a pointed one : ' It seems that where you are your aid is not required. Those who conduct that Government esteem themselves much abler to manage than you can advise. And, indeed, considering how opposite their end is to ours, I think they are right. Their abilities are exactly shaped to their purpose—the ruin of the empire. Let me, therefore, beseech you to come where you will be welcome and useful.' The voice of Congress, he assures Price, is the ' most honourable testimony of your merit ' ; and in inspiring words he tells him that ' It is the voice of wisdom which calls you to the noblest of all works— the assisting to form a government which means to make the principles of equal justice and the general rights the chief objects of its attention. Generations yet unborn

[1] *Journals of Congress*, vol. xii, pp. 984-5, a photostat of which, showing also how the representatives of the States voted on the motion, was kindly supplied to the author by the Librarian of the Library of Congress, Washington.

may bless the contributors to this inestimable work, and among them I trust the name of Dr. Price will hold a distinguished place.'[1] Extremely attractive though this pressing invitation to go to America to lay down the financial foundation of its constitution was, Price felt himself obliged to refuse it. On January 19, 1779, he wrote in reply from Newington Green : ' It is not possible for him to express the sense he has of the honour this resolution does him, and the satisfaction with which he reflects on the favourable opinion of him which has occasioned it ', at the same time giving as reasons for his refusal that ' he knows himself to be ill-qualified for giving such assistance, and he is also so connected in this country, and advancing so fast into the evening of life, that he cannot think of a removal '. He assures Congress, however, that he has great hopes of the new Republic : ' he looks to the United States as now the hope, and likely soon to become the refuge of mankind.'[2]

The American war was still going on, and though he had decided to become a ' silent spectator ', his refusal of the invitation of Congress did not mark quite the end of Price's relation to America. But before we note the few remaining events therein we must follow Price's activities in another field in the year 1778. In that year he published with his friend Priestley a philosophic discussion which they had been carrying on. The circumstances and nature of the discussion are fully explained in the Introduction to the work.

In 1777 there had appeared from the pen of Joseph Priestley a volume entitled *Disquisitions relating to Matter and Spirit*. Its dedication was dated ' Calne, July

---

[1] Morgan, *Memoirs*, pp. 78–9.
[2] Price's letter in Morgan, *Memoirs*, pp. 79–80.

1777 ', Priestley being then with Shelburne. In addition
to conducting scientific experiments while there he
wrote prolifically on metaphysical and theological
questions. His publications on these questions were very
unorthodox, some being considered even atheistical. The
Disquisitions was the chief of them. In order to proceed
' with the greatest caution in a business of such moment ',
he tells us, ' I desired some of my learned friends, and
especially Dr. Price, to peruse the work before it was
published.' [1] Price criticized it, and Priestley says that
' the remarks that he made upon it led to a free and
friendly discussion of the several subjects of it ' ; and
that these remarks were ' afterwards published jointly '.
Price left Priestley to manage the publication as he pleased;
so that it was Priestley who, in fact, saw the work through
the press.[2] It was entitled, *A Free Discussion of the
Doctrines of Materialism and Philosophical Necessity*, and
appeared in 1778. Priestley prides himself upon the fact
that it remains ' a proof of the possibility of discussing
subjects mutually considered as of the greatest importance
with the most perfect good-temper and without the least
diminution of friendship '. Price confirms this in very
similar words when he says that the work ' will afford
a proof that two persons may differ totally on points the
most important and sacred, with a perfect esteem for one
another ' ; and he expresses the opinion that ' it may
likewise give a specimen of a proper manner of carrying
on religious controversies '. The plan of the discussion
was Priestley's. In the introduction he explains that he
proposed that Price ' should re-write his remarks after
seeing what use I had already made of them in my sheet

[1] Thorpe, *Joseph Priestley*, p. 87.
[2] See Letter, ' Newington Green, May 14, 1778 ', prefixed to this
work.

of Illustrations; that I should then reply to them distinctly,
article by article, that he should remark, and I reply
again, till we should both be satisfied that we had done as
much justice as we could to our several arguments,
frankly acknowledging any mistakes we might be convinced of'. To this proposal Price 'cheerfully acquiesced'.
Priestley further acknowledges that in proposing this
scheme, he was not without a ' further view ', which was,
that among so many angry opponents as he expected, he
might secure a friendly one, ' and at the same time one
who could not but be acknowledged to be as capable of
doing ample justice to his argument as any writer of the
age'. Thus arose the *Free Discussion* which ranged over
the subjects of the Nature of Matter and the Human
Soul, the Mortality of the Soul and the Nature of the
Deity, and the Doctrine of Necessity. Both parties
show great zeal, but both, Priestley assures us, ' are
equally upright', the object of both being ' truth not
victory '.

The main point in dispute regarding matter is its being
or not being such as is capable of thought, Priestley
contending the former, and Price the latter. Price, deny-
ing that matter can think, argues for a soul separate from
the body. The powers of perception and thought reside
in an immaterial substance, but the exercise of these
powers depends on the organization of the body. Priestley,
placing these powers in the organized body itself, denies
the existence of a separate soul. Price can be convinced
' that there is no such thing as matter ', but he ' cannot
be convinced that there is no such thing as spirit '. By
spirit he means ' such a thinking, intelligent, nature as
I feel myself to be '.[1] Such a spirit or soul is a substance ;

---

[1] *Free Discussion*, p. 85.

and it is one : ' to divide the self would be to annihilate
it.' [1] The views of both Price and Priestley are coupled
with a belief in a resurrection and immortality. On the
perennial question of freedom, Price argues for it, Priestley
against it. Price's defence of liberty is excellent. Spirit
is necessarily self-determined. We must be ' agents ' or
' the proper and ultimate causes of our own actions '.
' Does it follow ', he asks, ' that because I am myself the
cause, there is no cause ? ' Liberty, he maintains, ' is
consistent with acting with a regard to motives ', for
' whoever acts means to do somewhat '.[2] The power of
determining ourselves, by the very nature of it ' wants an
end and rule to guide it ', hence ' no probability or
certainty of its being exerted agreeably to a rule can have
the least tendency to infringe or diminish it '.[3] Considered
in the light of the *Review*, whose philosophy is their
foundation, his contributions to these Discussions mark
Price as one of the most capable exponents of modern
Idealism.

A brief return to American matters came again. Whenever the Government proclaimed a Fast Price considered it
more as a political than a religious ordinance, and notwithstanding his never referring from the pulpit to
political topics on other days of religious worship he
always seized the opportunity offered by these Fast days
to deliver his opinions on the war. His name was now
a household word in the country, and his Sunday congregations had become regularly very large ; but even
those at their best were much exceeded by the massed
congregations that gathered to hear him, afire with passion
and zeal for liberty, justice, and peace, pour forth his
soul on these Fast days. February 10, 1779, was a Fast

---

[1] Ibid., p. 62.   [2] Ibid., p. 137.   [3] Ibid.

day.　Price preached an eloquent political sermon, which was afterwards published, at the Gravel Pit, Hackney. It echoes the sentiments of the two works on Civil Liberty. It re-asserts the sovereignty of the people.　The ' righteous citizen ', he claims, ' can have no notion of passive obedience and non-resistance '.　Price denies emphatically that resistance can be justified only in cases of extreme oppression :　' The truth is, oppression cannot be resisted too soon.'　To this sermon is added a postscript, in reply to Dr. Lowth, Bishop of London, who had attacked Price in a sermon preached on the preceding Ash Wednesday in the Chapel Royal.　The reply consists in showing that the Bishop had himself, formerly, expressed the very same sentiments and in almost exactly the same words as some of those uttered by Price.　The quotations from the Bishop's previous utterances, given by Price, are certainly such that it would be very difficult, without direction, to know whether they are taken from Price's own writings, or, as in fact they are, from Lowth.　' Heaven is angry with us ', says Price, and ' never did so dark a cloud hang over this nation '.　' May heaven avert the storm,' he again cries, ' or if it must break, may its fury be mitigated and the issue directed to the general advantage of the interest of truth, liberty, and virtue.'

February 21, 1781, was another Fast day.　Price preached at the Gravel Pit another political sermon in which he reviews his endeavours on behalf of America and liberty.　He admits that he was far from expecting that anything he could write would influence the managers of the affairs of his country.　He claims, however, that ' *had* they been influenced by it, this kingdom instead of being on the brink of ruin, would have been enjoying its former prosperity '.　Many of his representations, he reminds his hearers, which when written were appre-

hensions only, ' may now be read as history '. ' Events
have proved that I was right', he says triumphantly.
This being so, he points out how very improper had been
the ' load of abuse ' he had suffered.

He had not laboured, however, to receive nothing but
abuse. In addition to the marks of honour he had
already received both from his own country and from
America, he was now to receive more from the latter,
this time from its academical institutions. In 1781, the
University of Yale, one of the greatest not only in America,
but in the world, and founded by a Welshman, Elihu Yale,
conferred on him a great distinction. He and Washington,
then the commander-in-chief in the war that was still going
on, and soon to become the first President of the Republic,
were given the degree of LL.D. together, they being the
only ones to receive it on the occasion. ' At a meeting of
the Yale Corporation on April 24, 1781, it was voted to
confer the degree of Doctor of Laws upon George Washington and upon Richard Price.' [1] In a letter to Ezra Stiles,
President of Yale, dated ' September 29 ' of that year,
Price modestly acknowledges the honour, and pays a high
tribute to Washington : ' I hope Yale College, over
which you preside, will accept my warmest thanks for
this testimony of their approbation. I should be one
of the happiest of mankind, could I think that the account
given of me so handsomely in the diploma did not go

---

[1] Minute extract kindly supplied by the Secretary to the Secretary,
Yale University, New Haven, Connecticut. Again both Professor
T. Fowler, President of Corpus Christi, Oxford, in his article on
Price in the *Dictionary of National Biography*, 1896, and J. M.
Mitchell, in his article in the *Encyclopædia Britannica*, 11th ed.,
1910–11, are in error—the former as regards date, which he errone-
ously gives as 1783, and the latter as regards degree, which he
erroneously gives as D.D.

beyond any merit that I can justly claim. The circumstance mentioned in your letter, that the honour done me by the College was granted me at the same time with General Washington, has made a greater impression upon me than can be easily conceded. It is a circumstance that makes the honour distinguishing, beyond all that my ambition could reach to. General Washington's name must always shine among the first in the annals of the world.' [1] A few years later, Price was again brought into relationship with Yale. The philosophical apparatus of the College being very incomplete, Dr. Stiles, the President, ' availing himself of the friendship of Dr. Price, wrote to him for assistance in procuring this apparatus ', in 1787. Price readily complied with the request. He purchased the apparatus in London, bearing part of the expense, carefully attended to the quality of the several articles of which it was composed, and requested the College to accept it as ' a contribution ' from him, with his ' good will and respect '. By a vote of the Corporation, the President was asked to express to Price their ' most sensible gratitude ' for his ' generous liberality ' and ' very attentive and kind offices on this occasion '.[2]

In the following year, Price received yet another honour from America, being elected a Fellow of the American Academy of Arts and Sciences, Boston, on January 30, 1782.[3]

For some time Price had regarded this country as hurrying to its ruin. Shelburne shared his views. As far back as the Autumn of 1777, the year of the publication of the *Additional Observations*, Shelburne had expressed to

[1] Holmes, *The Life of Ezra Stiles*, pp. 287-8.

[2] Ibid., pp. 297-8.

[3] Fact and date kindly supplied by the Assistant Librarian of the Academy.

Price his anxiety.   Both rejoiced in the success of America, both deplored the prospect before this country.   ' America is safe,' says Shelburne, ' but my dear friend, what will become of England ? ' [1]   He was extremely intimate with Price, and in this letter, which conveys some confidential news, he confesses, ' When I write to you, my heart and pen go together '.   The friends of America then regarded Shelburne as the one person to bring the war to an end and so save England.   At that time Arthur Lee wrote to Price, ' If anyone can save a nation so pressed within and threatened without, it is our friend Lord Shelburne.' [2] A necessary first step was the fall of the North ministry. In 1780 a pamphlet attacking North's administration appeared anonymously.   Though the administration held on for another two years, this pamphlet served materially to bring about its fall.   It was entitled *Facts*, and, though published anonymously, was generally known to have been written by Horne Tooke and Price in collaboration.   It consisted of two parts, one of which, that by Price, dealt solely with the nation's finance. Among the many examples of waste that characterized the war were the shameful bargains that were made with various contractors for supplying the army and navy with stores and provisions.   Against these, and particularly against the notorious rum contract, Price's friends, and especially Colonel Isaac Barré, spoke with all their energy in the House of Commons.   It was to arouse the country to realize the wasteful and profligate way in which its resources were used that Price and Horne Tooke published *Facts*.   It ran to several editions in a few months.   The war continued till the following year, 1781, when, in

---

[1] Letter ' Bowood Park, Sept. 24, 1777 '.   In *Price Letters*.
[2] Letter ' Paris, April 20, 1777 '.   Ibid.

October, the British army capitulated to the American
army at Yorktown.   Early in 1782, Shelburne, then a
member of the Rockingham ministry which had succeeded
North's, ' opened unofficial negotiations ' with Benjamin
Franklin.   In July of that year he became Prime Minister,
and he immediately used all his powers to secure peace.
He succeeded in concluding it before the end of the year,
the Preliminary Articles being signed on November 30,
1782.   These were ratified in September 1783 by the
Treaty of Paris, whereby the Independence of the United
States was recognized.   So ended a war which Price had
watched with the greatest concern and anxiety from its
commencement, and it must have been a matter of
peculiar gratification to him that the peace which marked
its issue was negotiated by his best friends in both
countries.

Disappointed at not having Price as a citizen of the
United States, the Americans requested him to write
a pamphlet embodying such views and advice as he
would think fit to give in that form.   Dr. Rush, of Philadelphia, dwelling on the fact that the American Revolution was not over, and that only the first act of the drama
was finished, tells Price that ' it yet remains to effect
a revolution in our principles, opinions, and manners, so
as to accommodate them to the government we have
adopted '.   This, he realizes, is ' the most difficult part
of the business of the patriots of our country ', and it
' requires more wisdom and fortitude than to expel or
reduce armies into captivity '.   And this most important
work, he also realizes, there is one man more fitted than
all others to do. ' I wish to see this idea inculcated by
your pen ', is his confession to Price.   ' Call upon the
rulers of your country to lay the foundation of their
empire in knowledge as well as virtue.   This will render

the American revolution a blessing to mankind. As you
have staked your reputation upon this great event with
the world and with posterity, you must not desert us
till you see the curtain drop and the last act of the drama
closed. A small pamphlet addressed by you to the
Congress and the Legislatures of each of the States, would,
I am sure, have more weight with our rulers than an
hundred publications thrown out by the citizens of this
country.'[1] This last statement is a truly remarkable
testimony to the enormous influence Price had in America,
especially when we remember what very able and eminent
men those citizens comprised. Price gave the advice
sought in the form of an Address to the People of the
United States in a small pamphlet entitled, *Observations
on the Importance of the American Revolution, and the
Means of making it a Benefit to the World*. It was printed
in this country in 1784, and distributed in America in
the same year. It was not distributed in this country
at the time. Its author even directed, when it was printing, that ' no extracts may yet be made from this
pamphlet '.[2] Both the printing and the publication of
it were at Price's expense.[3] It deals with the best means
of securing those liberties which had already been won,
and recommends to the States, among other things, the
establishment of a Sinking Fund, the cultivation of peace,
and the formation of a strict political union among
themselves on which their credit, liberties, and existence
even, depended. Liberty of conscience and of speech,
the civil establishment of religion, education, property,
trade, banks, oaths, the negro trade, and slavery are also
considered at some length. It had a great reception.

---

[1] Morgan, *Memoirs*, pp. 104–5.
[2] *Gentleman's Magazine*, vol. liv, Pt. 2, p. 927.   [3] Ibid.

Franklin thought it ' excellent '. Dr. Wheelock, of
Dartmouth College, writing in August 1785, told Price,
' Your observations on the importance of the American
Revolution I have had the pleasure to read with particular
attention. I cannot tell you how great the applause is
which its author receives throughout these states.' The
President of one of the Legislatures, he further says,
' wrote a letter to the Assembly at their session last
February, including the *Observations*. He informed the
Legislature that the remarks of the pamphlet were the
best legacy which he could leave them. He prayed
earnestly that the spirit of them might animate the
manners and dispositions of legislators and people to the
last age.'

It is quite clear that in these critical early years of its
existence, America looked to Price, as to the ablest of
its own citizens, to guide its destiny. Whether in respect
of the philosophical justification of those principles which
were at once the foundation and the driving power of
the Revolution and the very life of the Republic, or in
respect of that practical, sound, financial policy which
is one of the conditions of the prosperity of any state,
the very highest value was placed upon the views and
counsels of Richard Price. Even after the distribution
of the ' pamphlet of Advice ' as Franklin termed the last
Observations, we find Price still exhorted to continue his
' benevolent exertions to ameliorate and enlighten the
people, and to arouse them to improve and perfect their
several forms of government '. ' No man living ', says
the writer, ' can influence them as much as you can.' [1]
Price did continue to take a live interest in the affairs

---

[1] William Hazlitt, from Hollywell, 18 Nov. 1785. In *Price
Letters*.

of America, and jealously to guard its rights, as is shown by James Sullivan, the first President of the Massachusetts Historical Society, telling him, ' You were very kind in giving me liberty to communicate to you anything respecting infringements upon the sacred rights of conscience which might happen in our Commonwealth.' He, also, testifies to the trust reposed in Price : ' There is no one, Sir, on the globe to whom I should apply myself in difficulties of this sort sooner than to you.' The matter in question was safe, however, for his correspondent continues : ' I am very happy to inform you that the Judges of our Supreme Judicial Court have given at last such a construction to our declaration of rights as sets this point upon a liberal and safe footing.' We must note that in this matter, again, a letter written by Price was an influencing factor. ' I shall not do you justice ', says the same writer, ' without observing that I believe your letter did much towards it.' [1]

One more academic honour came to him. On January 22, 1785, he was elected a Fellow of the American Philosophical Society, Philadelphia.[2]

Price took no further direct part in the affairs of America.

[1] Letters from James Sullivan, Boston, 16 Oct., 1786. In *Price Letters*.

[2] Fact and date kindly supplied by the Assistant Secretary of the Society.

CHAPTER VII

MOVEMENTS aiming at advancement and reform, in
whatever field, always found in Price an influential and
enthusiastic supporter.   In the eighties of the century
he was a zealous and moving spirit in the promotion of
worthy ends in diverse fields.   Theology, politics, education, and religious freedom, all claimed him alike in that
decade.

In September 1783 a Society was instituted ' for
promoting the knowledge of the Scriptures ', its meetings
being held in Essex House, the home of Unitarianism.
Among the names of the original members we find that
of ' Dr. Price '.   The Society limited its aim to the
interpretation of the Scriptures, and declined all contributions which were ' wholly controversial ' or which
were ' formal defences or confutations of special doctrines '.
The method of interpretation fixed upon proceeded ' by
settling the text by a comparison of various readings, by
accurate translation, division and punctuation, by a
concise, well-digested commentary, by notes, philological
and explanatory, and finally, by adding doctrinal and

moral conclusions '.[1] The Society, however, though it had among others such men as Law, Bishop of Carlisle, and Priestley, as Price's fellow-members, did not flourish, and after a few years' existence it was disbanded. In fact its plan overlapped that of the *Theological Repository*, which drew its support from much the same source, and which, having itself also lapsed for some time, had by then been resumed. The Society left a legacy of a few commentaries and translations, but Price did not produce anything under its auspices.

The year 1785 saw Price once more engaged in seeking to improve Parliamentary Representation at home. The evil of the distribution of seats had become greatly accentuated with the rise during the Industrial Revolution of new and large towns which had no representation whatsoever. There existed ' pocket boroughs ', whose representatives were nominated by a peer or by the Crown; and ' rotten boroughs '—like Old Sarum, which returned two members although it had only two voters— which were created merely to add, through their representation, to the power of the Crown; and the selling of seats by public auction. These evils called aloud for reform in Price's day, and he was always in the van of the reformers. With the question of representation Price always associated that of the duration of Parliament. For him the Septennial Act of 1716, extending the life of Parliament to seven years, was a blow to liberty, for it increased the independence of the representatives, and proportionately lessened the authority of the people. ' Shorter Parliaments ' became a popular cry. Price attacked the whole evil on every available opportunity. He had focussed attention on it by means of his *Civil*

---

[1] Belsham, *Memoirs of Theophilus Lindsay*, pp. 131–2.

Liberty, and although he was not concerned in any public attempt at reform after 1785, he urged its necessity again in 1789 and 1790. Always he spoke of representation, both in its extent and in its duration, in terms of liberty. He was actively associated with all the attempts at reform made during his lifetime. He was a powerful supporter of those made by Wilkes in 1776, by the Duke of Richmond in 1780, and by Pitt in 1782, 1783, and 1785. Not until 1832, however, was reform secured.

When Price's friend, Lord Shelburne, became Prime Minister, in 1782, he offered the office of Chancellor of the Exchequer to William Pitt, the younger, then a young man of twenty-three. In December of that year the King's speech contained a reference, worded by Price, to the necessity for improving the country's finances. About that time Shelburne offered to Price the post of private secretary, which, as might be expected, he refused. The post was little suited to his habits and disposition, and at no time had his friendship with Shelburne been based on the least motive of private interest, and it would have been great condescension rather than any aspiration on his part to accept. His expert advice on financial and other matters would still be at the disposal of Shelburne. His friend, however, was not destined to hold his high office long. In February of the following year Shelburne resigned, being succeeded by the Fox-North coalition, which, in its turn, fell before the end of the year. The opportunity was Pitt's, who, though not yet twenty-five, was entrusted with the task of forming a Government. Having no majority in the House when he took office, he adopted the procedure of clinging to office until he thought the moment favourable for an appeal to the country. That moment came in 1784, and Pitt was returned by a large majority. After his accession Pitt had one great ambition

—the redemption of the national debt. He had proposals of his own, but before putting them into operation he submitted them, in 1786, to the judgement of Price, soliciting from him any improvement he could suggest, or ' any other proposal which from your knowledge of the subject you may think preferable '. ' When you have had sufficient time to consider them I should be greatly obliged to you if you will allow me to hope for the pleasure of seeing you at any time that is convenient to you.' [1] The principle of Pitt's proposals, based upon the conversion of the three per cents into five per cents, was one which Price himself had often publicly urged and which he had repeated in his private communications to Pitt. But it was so misapplied by Pitt that Price ' very strongly urged his objections ' to his proposals. A week later Pitt wrote to Price admitting that his objections were ' on the whole very convincing '. ' I shall think myself obliged to you,' said Pitt, ' if you would do me the honour to call any morning after Tuesday next in Downing-Street . . . I am anxious to avail myself to the utmost of your assistance where it may be so material.' [2] The outcome of the interview was that Pitt was so far convinced of the weakness of his proposals as to request Price to submit to him a plan of his own. Price submitted three plans, with ' a very considerable recommendation of the first plan ', on the strength of the particular vigour with which it would have operated at its outset, ' when vigour was most wanted.' Pitt, however, seems to have adopted the third and weakest plan ' from an apprehension, if he adopted either of the two other plans, that he should be obliged to load the country, in the course of five years, with new

[1] Letter to Price, dated ' 8th of January, 1786 ' in *Reversionary Payments*, 3rd ed., vol. i, pp. 318–19.
[2] Ibid.

taxes to the amount of half a million '. He firmly believed
that even that plan would answer his purpose well. In
the great speech which he made on its introduction he
predicted that the Sinking Fund would so reduce the
National Debt ' that the exigencies of war would never
again raise it to its former enormous height ', and he
' looked upon this as his chief title to fame '.[1] ' This
plan,' he said, ' which I have now the honour to bring
forward, has long been the wish and hope of all men, and
I am proud to flatter myself that my name may be
inscribed on that firm column now about to be raised to
national faith and national prosperity.' Yet Pitt did not
mention Price's name when he presented the plan, nor
did he make public the least acknowledgement of the
advice he had sought and received from Price. The
Sinking Fund did not in fact prove to be an effective
means of clearing off the Debt. On the contrary, the latter
increased very considerably during Pitt's administration.
Pitt is ' the minister in all English history who has thrown
the heaviest burden upon posterity '.[2] The reason is
twofold. Price's third plan was no doubt so far fallacious
that ' the interest of the capitalised stock devoted to
the payment of the debt' was 'not a spontaneous product ',
but ' exclusively derived from taxation appropriated to
the purpose ', and that therefore it was ' by taxation,
and taxation alone ', that the debt was paid.[3] Again,
Pitt seems to have applied the plan imperfectly. The
' case against the financial administration of Pitt ', says
Lecky, ' is overwhelming '.[4] Those defenders of Pitt
who are unwilling to accept the view of Pitt's relationship

---

[1] Lecky, *History of England in the Eighteenth Century*, vol. v, pp.
53–4.

[2] Ibid., vol. v, pp. 53–4.

[3] Ibid., vol. v, p. 51.   [4] Ibid., vol. v, p. 53.

with Price which Lecky and others accept, apparently have no evidence to refute it. The latest defence of Pitt [1] neither proves Pitt's independence of Price in the matter of the scheme he submitted to Parliament—which is certainly necessary in view of his several consultations with Price on that very matter—nor justifies Pitt's complete forgetfulness of the adviser whose judgement he solicited and received. Price's fears regarding the Debt were premature, it is true, and he was mistaken in thinking that it was impossible that the establishment of the Sinking Fund should become the means of increasing the Debt. He also greatly underrated the resources of the country, and quite as greatly overrated the powers of compound interest. Two things remain true, however. First, whatever merit is usually attributed to Pitt for having established, or, strictly, re-established, the Sinking Fund, that merit really belongs to Price, inasmuch as Pitt was nothing more than a convert to Price's insistent and consistent teaching on the subject. Price's friend, the Marquis of Lansdowne—to which rank Shelburne had been raised on November 30, 1784, he being the first to carry the Lansdowne title—speaks the simple truth when he tells Price ' as long as a sinking fund exists . . . your name must be connected with it '.[2] And secondly, though Price's contribution to this sphere of finance does not compare with his other work on annuities in the fields of Life Insurance and Old Age Pensions, and does not warrant the disproportionate view that Price is ' *chiefly remembered* as the author of the Sinking Fund Scheme afterwards adopted by Pitt ',[3] yet he did valuable service

---

[1] J. Holland Rose, *Life of Pitt*, pp. 190–3.

[2] ' Bowood Park, 29th Sept. 1786.' In *Price Letters*.

[3] *Dictionary of Political Economy*, vol. iii, p. 189 ; Art. by H. E. Egerton. Italics are ours.

in leading the public and the Government alike seriously to face the question of the redemption of the Debt.

Ever since the year following her marriage, Price's wife had been more or less an invalid. A paralytic disorder, though slight in its first attack, had in the course of two years considerably impaired her faculties and rendered her incapable of deriving much enjoyment either from reading or from conversation. She had, however, so far recovered her strength and spirits as to be capable of enjoying the society of her friends. The purity of her mind and the benevolence of her disposition had well fitted her to be Price's companion. During the last five years her illness increased, an event which caused Price to retire from one of his pastorates. He relinquished that of Newington Green in 1783, retaining henceforth only that of the Gravel Pit, Hackney. His wife died on September 20, 1786. She was buried in Bunhill Fields in the same grave as Samuel Price, her husband's uncle. Her loss was as deeply felt and as sincerely lamented by him as if no malady had reconciled him to its approach. They had lived together very happily for nearly thirty years. He tells his sister, Mrs. Morgan, of his ' inexpressible anguish at this separation after thirty years of uninterrupted happiness '. The news of her death having been communicated to his friend, the Marquis of Lansdowne, the latter wrote to him from Bowood Park a very affectionate letter. The Marquis had himself had several experiences of domestic bereavement, which ' though they have hurt my health fundamentally ', yet ' have made me a better and for that reason a happier man '. This fact and his great friendship for Price explain the sensitive response and sincere sympathy which his letter reveals. ' Tho' the post allows me but a moment ', says he, ' I cannot delay a day to assure you that you

have not a relation who feels more sensibly the loss you
have sustain'd. I have no need when I write to you,
particularly on this occasion, to wait for reflection ; I am
not afraid to let my heart dictate. Let me beseech you
to command me in any shape. I will go instantly to
London, if I can contribute to your comfort, or will be
happy to see you here where no one shall come but such
as are agreeable to you.' [1] A few days later, on the 29th,
Lansdowne repeats his invitation : ' If you will venture
here . . . you will find Lady Lansdowne and me nearly
alone for two months to come. . . . We'll treat you as
a father. Every person about the house reveres and
respects you, and you'll make us very happy, which is
the next best thing to being happy yourself.' [2] Whether
or not Price went to the home where he was so often
a beloved guest, we know that he went for a few weeks
to his nephew William Morgan, the Actuary, who was then
living at Sydenham. But his distress of mind while there
was such that he could never be persuaded to revisit
that place. Nor could he ever enter the burial-ground
where his wife's remains lay, without great agitation.
Several of his friends found it necessary to urge him to
exert himself. Lansdowne counselled him to the same
purpose on two occasions. To his uncle in this affliction
came William Morgan's brother, George Cadogan Morgan,
from Yarmouth, whither he had newly gone from Norwich,
where he had been minister of the congregation worshipping in the famous Octagon chapel, and Price found ' the
greatest comfort in his good sense, good nature, and
vivacity ', and expressed the hope that ' some event or
other will be the means of bringing him to reside in

---

[1] ' Bowood Park, Sept. 21, 1786 '. In *Price Letters*.
[2] ' Bowood Park, Sept. 29, 1786 '. Ibid.

London '. Morgan did not delay in gratifying his uncle's wish. Before the year was out, he removed to the neighbourhood of London ' to undertake the education of young men of liberal families', and he soon had quite as many pupils as he could receive in the house he took at Southgate— a short distance from Stamford Hill, then quite rural, where his brother William was building one of the first houses on the hill, only a hedge separating it from the house which another financial genius, one of the Rothschilds, had there.

It was a good thing for Price that in the year of his sorrow a movement was begun in which he was greatly interested. It was a movement to establish in or near London a new Dissenting Academy.[1] A ' respectable meeting of a number of Protestant Dissenters ', presided over by Thomas Rogers, considered it of the greatest importance that proper Seminaries should be established ' on liberal principles ' for the education of their Ministers. The dissolution of the Academies at Hoxton, Warrington, and Exeter made the need urgent, ' the Academy at Daventry alone being inadequate to the exigencies of the situation '. The desire was for an Academy where students would not necessarily be taught the orthodox view on the subject of the Trinity. Even Hoxton, established as it had been under the Trust of Mr. Coward, who was a strong Calvinist and Trinitarian, had long ceased to teach the orthodox view. Warrington and Exeter had likewise become unorthodox. It was this desire to safeguard ' liberal principles ' that was given first place in a letter,

---

[1] The whole account given here is taken from *Resolutions and Proceedings relating to the Establishment of a new Academical Institution among Protestant Dissenters in the Vicinity of London, in the year 1786.* It is surprising that Parker's *Dissenting Academies in England* makes no mention of this one in its appended list of Academies.

dated ' February 14, 1786 ', sent out over the names of
the Committee, of which Price was the most important
member, asking for support. This letter speaks of giving
students such an education as shall best ' assist them in
judging for themselves, improve them in valuable knowledge, guard them against bigotry, and prejudices, and
at the same time form their characters to a rational piety
and zeal '. The movement was regarded as ' the greatest
occasion ' which had ever called forth the attention and
the ardour of liberal-minded Protestant Dissenters, and
' one of the greatest occasions ' that had ever been
presented to the friends of truth and piety, and of civil
and religious liberty. Several of the Trustees of Warrington and Exeter supported the plan, and liberal contributions were promised by members of the public. These
promises amounted to over seven thousand pounds in
donations and over six hundred pounds in annual sub-
scriptions. No divinity students were to be admitted
under sixteen years of age, and no lay students under
fifteen or over eighteen. On the last Wednesday in
April an annual Sermon was to be preached before the
friends of the institution by an appointed minister ' on
some subject relating to religious liberty, the rights of
private judgement, or other fundamental principles of the
Institution '. Until suitable accommodation was decided
upon, the Trustees of Dr. Daniel Williams, of whom Price
was one, granted the use of a room at the library. The
' Academical business commenced in the beginning of
October, 1786, with five divinity students besides one
who is on his own foundation '. Soon after, a house was
purchased in Hackney into which the Institution moved on
September 29, 1787. From that date, the Academy was
known as the ' New College, Hackney '. Dr. Abraham
Rees, who had acted as ' Superintending Resident Tutor '

while the Institution was in the temporary premises, was
appointed to the office of ' Resident Tutor ' and ' to take
the direction and government of the Institution '.

The Sermon on the occasion of its actual opening in
1786 was delivered by Dr. Andrew Kippis ; that on the
occasion of the more formal opening on Wednesday, the
25th of April 1787, by Price, who had removed to Hackney
a month before. Both Sermons were preached at the
Old Jewry, where Dr. Abraham Rees was pastor, and
published, each in the year of its delivery. That by Price
appeared under the title, ' The Evidence for a Future
Period of Improvement in the State of Mankind, with the
Means and Duty of Promoting it.' It is really a Discourse
on Educational Ideals. Price holds before his hearers the
hopeful expectation that ' there is a progressive improvement in human affairs which will terminate in greater
degrees of light and virtue and happiness than have yet
been known '. He urges the infinite perfectibility of
mankind, for there are not ' any limits beyond which
knowledge and improvement cannot be carried '. As to
the means whereby this ' happy termination of affairs
on this globe ' is to be realized, Price says that ' it is
obvious that this end is to be brought about by the
operation of Providence concurring with those tendencies
to improvement . . . observed to be inseparable from the
nature of man '. These tendencies are best to be seen in
' the investigations and active exertions of enlightened
and honest men '. The objects of education are ' catholi-
cism, virtue, and rational piety ', together with ' a spirit
of candour and benevolence '. He lays it down that
' nothing is very important except an honest mind ;
nothing fundamental except righteous practice and a
sincere desire to know and do the will of God '. It is by
its provision of such an education that Price wishes

New College to be known. Would that events had justified the high expectations entertained of it !

A passage in this Sermon deserves special notice in view of Price's efforts after Parliamentary Reform, and as a comment on them. Claiming to speak for the whole body of Protestant Dissenters, Price denies that their agitation for reform is an agitation for a Republic, and declares that what they demand is a pure and vigorous administration of the Constitution they have. ' I cannot help taking this opportunity ', he says, ' to remove a very groundless suspicion with respect to myself, by adding that so far am I from preferring a government purely republican, that I look upon our own constitution of Government as better adapted than any other to this country, and in theory excellent.' [1]

The College was a Presbyterian College, being intended, Price says, mainly for the education of those belonging to the denomination ' to which we belong ', explaining that he speaks of ' the Presbyterian denomination of dissenters only '. The curriculum was a very wide one, and included ' the Latin, Greek and Hebrew Languages, Greek and Roman Antiquities, Ancient and Modern Geography, Universal Grammar, Rhetoric and Composition, Chronology, History—Civil and Ecclesiastical—the Principles of Law and Government, the several branches of Mathematics, Astronomy, Natural and Experimental Philosophy and Chemistry, Logic, Metaphysics, and Ethics, the Evidences of Religion—Natural and Revealed—Theology, Jewish Antiquities, and Critical Lectures on the Scriptures '. The tutors were ' Rev. Richard Price, D.D., F.R.S., Rev. Andrew Kippis, D.D., F.R.S. and F.S.A., Rev. Abraham Rees, D.D., F.R.S., Rev. Hugh Worthing-

---

[1] Cf. a passage in a Letter, 1790, quoted below, p. 136.

ton, Rev. George Cadogan Morgan, and Rev. John
Kiddle '. There was also to be a special tutor for Elocution.
The first two members of the Staff named were extremely
busy men, and it appears they had been prevailed upon
to take up their offices more because of the status they
gave to the College than on account of any great amount
of time they could devote to them. Price's subjects were
' select parts of Morals, Mathematics, Astronomy, and
Natural Philosophy '. He did not continue long to give
this assistance in the tutorial work, though he remained
to the end of his days a liberal financial supporter.
Kippis, too, held his tutorship for only a short time.
Both he and Rees had been assistant tutors at the Hoxton
Academy. George Cadogan Morgan, the nephew whom
Price had already had the satisfaction of seeing coming to
London, was a scientist of very considerable attainments.
He had carried out valuable researches in the then young
science of electricity and made many original contributions to it. ' Poor Morgan ! ' says Rogers, ' he will
certainly die of some experiment.' Each session commenced on the third Monday in September and closed
on the first day of July. The fees were six guineas,
which included ' apartments, board, and education ', for
the session. Instruction in French and other Modern
Languages, Drawing, &c., were provided for an extra
fee. In August 1789, Thomas Belsham, who had since
1781 been tutor at Daventry, but who had resigned
from that office as well as from that of pastor of the
Independent congregation in that town, in 1788, upon
his conversion to Unitarianism, joined the staff as tutor
in Divinity, and remained so connected with it ' for the
last seven years of its existence '.[1] In 1791, Priestley, who

---

[1] Belsham, *Memoirs of Rev. Theophilus Lindsey*, pp. 216, 224.

had come to London, ' voluntarily and gratuitously undertook to deliver to the students at the College his admirable lectures upon history and chemistry '.[1] In 1790, Gilbert Wakefield, a second wrangler at the age of twenty, once a curate, and later a tutor at the Warrington Academy, joined the staff, but partly owing to his not frequenting any place of public worship, he resigned therefrom at the end of his first session, in 1791.[2]

Owing to mismanagement of the funds, New College was soon in difficulties. At Michaelmas, 1789, that is, only three years after the opening, there were only seventy pounds in hand to meet a debt of over six thousand pounds, plus the interest on this at the rate of six and a half per cent.[3] Belsham says the cause of the failure was the ' unfortunate purchase of the estate at Hackney '.[4] After a brief existence of ten years, the College had to be closed in 1796. Among those who were educated there during the ten years of its existence were Michael Maurice, father of Frederick Denison Maurice, who came over from the closed Hoxton Academy,[5] William Hazlitt, the celebrated essayist, and John Jones, LL.D, who went up from Christ College, Brecon, and who became tutor at the Carmarthen Presbyterian College during 1792–5 when it was located at Swansea.[6]

Price, we have just mentioned, had now removed from Newington Green, where he had spent nearly thirty years, to Hackney, where he had spent the first year of his married life. This was in March, 1787. His new abode

[1] Ibid., p. 225.
[2] Turner, *Lives of Eminent Unitarians*, vol. ii, p. 257.
[3] *Gentleman's Magazine* for 1790 ; vol. lx, Pt. 2, p. 793.
[4] Belsham, *Memoirs of Rev. Theophilus Lindsey*, p. 217.
[5] *Life of Frederick Denison Maurice*, by his Son ; vol. i, p. 7.
[6] See Jeremy, *The Presbyterian Fund*, pp. 194–5.

was St. Thomas's Square. Lansdowne had urged upon him the necessity of his getting some of his relations to live with him, for, he tells him, ' you must not live alone '.[1] Price soon took this course. His sister, Mrs. Morgan, had been a widow since the death of her husband, William Morgan, in Bridgend, in 1772. Her son and daughter, William Morgan, the Actuary, and his sister Nancy Morgan, had been living in London for some years, Nancy keeping house for her brother, as we have seen, at Black-friars Bridge. Both had now married. Mrs. Morgan, accompanied by her only unmarried daughter, Sally, now came to London to keep house for Price. He was suffering visibly in health, many ailments now undermining it. He was unable to take his daily riding exercise before dinner or take his cold bath two or three times weekly, as he had been accustomed to do for over forty years. His correspondence, which had for years been very heavy, was now irksome to him. He was greatly distressed, too, at losing friends. He used to regard the loss of friends as one of Providence's most effective means to wean our own interest from this world and so prepare us also to leave it.

In 1787, the year in which he published the sermon he preached on the formal opening of New College, Price published some of the sermons he had preached on Christian Doctrine to his congregation at Hackney. It was to them, who had requested their publication, that he dedicated *Sermons on the Christian Doctrine as received by the different Denominations of Christians*. With the Sermons dealing strictly with Doctrine were included ' Sermons on the Security and Happiness of a Virtuous Course, on the Goodness of God, and the Resurrection of

[1] ' Sept. 29, 1787.' In *Price Letters.*

Lazarus '. The Sermons on Doctrine are an exposition of Arianism, but not intended to be in any sense controversial. Price wards off controversy in a short Advertisement : ' I shall make no reply to any animadversions on the account which . . . I have given of the Doctrines of Christianity ; except by acknowledging the mistakes into which I may have fallen when convinced of them.' No controversy followed. The volume was well received. Lansdowne read it with warm approval. The first Sermon, which shows that, in spite of all differences, Christians ' are agreed in all that is essential ', he told Price ' should not only be read but *taught* in every school of every sect in England '. ' Children ', he said, ' should learn to spell out of it.' [1] Of the Sermon on ' The Happiness of a Virtuous Course ', he wrote, ' I never read thirty pages of any book whatever more happily expressed, or with which I was more captivated.' [2] Sir William Jones, the English Cato, celebrated Judge and Orientalist, pioneer of the study of Sanskrit in England, and founder of the Asiatic Society, also admired the volume as he did its author : ' I have lately ', he writes to his friend Price, ' read with delight a work in which all Christians are interested ; a volume of Sermons published by you, and showing the goodness both of your heart and of your head.' [3] The sermons on Doctrine, expound three ' schemes ', two ' extreme ' schemes and a ' middle ' scheme. The extreme schemes are Calvinism, on the one hand, and Socinianism, on the other, to both of which Price is opposed. The true scheme is the middle one, which is Arianism. Price's Arianism is nearer Socinianism than it is to Calvinism. He was a ' low ' Arian.[4] His

---

[1] Letter, ' B. P., 19 Dec. 1786.' In *Price Letters*.   [2] Ibid.
[3] ' Crishna Nagur, Sept. 26, 1788.' In Morgan, *Memoirs*, p. 115.
[4] See p. 66 *supra*.

friend Priestley, who was a Socinian, tells Price of his
[i. e. Priestley's] ' passing from Trinitarianism to high
Arianism, from this to your low Arianism, and from this to
Socinianism.[1] Arians and Socinians opposed each other
with zeal but always with toleration. There were several
points of difference, the outstanding one being the
doctrine of the pre-existence of Christ, which the former
asserted and the latter denied. As against Calvinists and
Trinitarians generally, Arians held that the Son was
a created Being not co-eternal with the Father ; while
as against Socinians, who held that the Son was a mere
man, Arians held that the Son existed before his appearance in the flesh. Doctrinal differences did not, any
more than philosophical differences, affect in the least
the friendship and mutual respect of Price and Priestley.
The latter dedicated one of his most challenging doctrinal
works [2] to Price ' as a mark of our friendship, and of
our love of the same studies '. In 1788, the year after
the publication of the *Sermons on Christian Doctrine*,
Price had some correspondence with Theophilus Lindsey,
the father of Unitarianism, who, like Priestley, Dr.
Lardner, Dr. Jebb, and Thomas Belsham, was an acknowledged Socinian. In his *Vindiciae Priestleianae*, Lindsey
coupled Price with the more orthodox Butler as having
held similar views with him of the nature and dignity of
Christ, and as having ' fallen into and adhered . . . fixedly
to this gloomy and unscriptural doctrine that repentance
alone is not sufficient to restore sinful mortals to the
favour of their Maker '.[3] Price, resenting this, wrote to
Lindsey correcting him : ' If contrary to my apprehen-

[1] Andrew Fuller, *The Calvinistic and Socinian Systems*, p. 279.
[2] *Critical Dissertations*, prefixed to a Harmony of the Evangelists ;
Letter of Dedication.
[3] *Vindiciae Priestleianae*, p. 249.

Hackney June 2 1786

Dear Sir

Accept my best thanks for your kind letter. It is entirely satisfactory to me, and leaves in my mind no room for any other sentiment than those of affection and respect wch I have always entertained for you. If my letter discovers any degree of unreasonable sensibility I hope you will forgive me. Indeed I care not what strong expressions of dislike are apply'd to my opinions concerning Christ provided they are properly represented, and I am not understood to hold that he is almost equal to the Supreme God; a sentiment at wch I shudder, and which probably no Arian now holds. I am oblig'd to you for the extract from Mr Freeman's letter. Deliver my kind and respectful remembrance to Mrs Lindsey. Wishing you and her all possible happiness I am truly and affectionately yours

Rich: Price

FACSIMILE OF RICHARD PRICE'S HANDWRITING

From a MS. in the private possession of Mr. Stephen K. Jones, Sub-Librarian of Dr. Williams's Library, London

sions the Socinian doctrine is true, I wish you success in
your endeavours to propagate it ; but whether true or
not, good must be done by all fair and candid discussions
of it. You have done me honour in joining me to Dr.
Butler ; but will you excuse me if I tell you that I am
sorry that, in your animadversions on him, you have not
intimated that I do not think as he does on the subject
of worshipping Christ, and that I have given an account
of the divine character and government, and human life,
very different from that which you censure ? I am
afraid that from your not distinguishing between him and
me, those who read you only will be led to very wrong
ideas of my sentiments on these points, and also on the
dignity of Christ and our redemption by Him.' ' My
convictions generally ', declares Price, ' are only a pre-
ponderance on one side, attended with a feeling of
difficulties ; and I am often ready to wish I was more
assured of the truth of my opinions.' ' But ', he goes on,
' in forming this wish I am checked by reflecting that this
assurance is most enjoyed by those who are most in the
wrong, Trinitarians, Calvinists, Papists, &c.' [1] Lindsey
immediately sent a reply, assuring Price that ' there is
no one living ' for whom he had greater respect and esteem,
expressing regret for having written anything needing
correction, and promising to make the correction in the
second part to be published later. Price was satisfied
with the reply, and in his turn sent his friend the assurance
' it is extremely satisfactory to me, and leaves in my mind
no room for any other sentiment than those of affection
and respect which I have always entertained for you '.
' I care not ', he declares, ' what strong expressions of

[1] Letter, ' Hackney, May 26, 1788 ', in the private possession of
Mr. Stephen K. Jones, Sub-Librarian, Dr. Williams's Library,
London, who kindly lent it to the author.

dislike are applied to my opinions concerning Christ, provided they are properly represented, and I am not understood to hold that he is *almost equal to the Supreme God*, a sentiment at which I shudder, and which probably no Arian now holds.' [1]

Arianism, from that of Clarke, foremost in its propagation in the latter half of the seventeenth century, to the somewhat different form of it advocated by Price, was never more than a passing phase of English theological thought. That it was very generally accepted within both Anglican and Dissenting Churches during that period is undeniable. Reflecting, no doubt, the influence of Price, congregation after congregation in long succession became Arian in Wales, most of them, as was the case with similar congregations in England also, only to revert before the close of the eighteenth century to their former beliefs, while the remainder, as Arianism waned, settled down as Unitarian churches. With the exception of its having given us a few Unitarian churches, Arianism has left no permanent mark upon our religious life.[2]

During these last years of the eighties, Price was much occupied with attempts to repeal the Test Act and so secure for Dissenters a large measure of freedom. No attempt at repeal had been made since Price was a youth. Now three attempts were made, and Price was prominently connected with each, but none of them was successful. The first attempt was made in 1787, when the hopes of the Dissenters were running high, partly owing to the extensive support which they had given to the young

---

[1] Letter, ' Hackney, June 2, 1788 ', in the private possession of Mr. Stephen K. Jones, Sub-Librarian, Dr. Williams's Library, London, who kindly lent it to the author.

[2] Its interesting history may be read in Colligan, *The Arian Movement in England*.

Pitt on his appeal to the country after accepting the Premiership, and partly owing to their entrusting the cause to Mr. Beaufoy, a member of the Established Church and a sturdy supporter of the Ministry. It was Beaufoy who championed the cause again in 1789, when the majority against it was very small. When the third attempt was made in 1790, Fox, who had supported Beaufoy, and was in turn supported by him, took charge of the Bill. His advocacy unfortunately gave to it a more distinctly party colour. But the event which had completely changed the whole aspect of the question was the outbreak of the Revolution in France, to which the Dissenters generally were favourable. Not only was the Bill rejected, but opinion was so strong against the Dissenters that no attempt at repeal was made again for nearly forty years, when Lord John Russell secured repeal in 1828.

CHAPTER VIII

Conditions in France — Outbreak of the French Revolution — opinion in England and Germany — Price rejoices in the Revolution — The ' Revolution Society ' — Price's Sermon on *The Love of Our Country* — which makes a profound impression — Burke replies with his *Reflections* — to which Paine replies with his *Rights of Man* — Revolution Society Dinner — Price proposes a Toast — Address transmitted to the French National Assembly — Price the ' Apostle of Liberty ' — marks of approval from French Societies — The ' Constitutional Society ' and its Dinner — Price toasted as ' The Friend of the Universe ' — A new Commemoration Society and its Dinner — Price proposes a Toast — Revolution Society Dinner — Price proposes a Toast — Price not an advocate for a Republic in England.

WE have now reached the year in which one of the greatest events in the history of the world occurred. Of all the events with which Price was concerned, none moved him more than the French Revolution. Its outbreak, in 1789, raised his hopes to their highest point, and he regarded it as an unmixed blessing. He did not live to see its later development : his estimate of it, the reader must realize, must be understood as applying only to its very initial stages.

The conditions that were a factor in bringing it about were social and economic. Those conditions, however, bad as they were, would probably not of themselves have produced a revolution. The conditions of the peasant in Germany and Spain were even worse than those prevailing in France.[1] The difference lay in the fact that in France the conditions were accompanied by the prevalence

[1] Green, *Short History*, vol. ii, p. 747.

of new ideas. France had got into touch with America, and its Government had in 1778 formed an alliance with the Republic across the sea. For more than ten years a channel had been open along which ideas about liberty and equality were flowing into France. Besides, there had been steadily growing for half a century in France a political philosophy which was spreading and popularizing there the ideas which Locke had taught, half a century earlier still, as the justification of the Revolution of 1688 in England—the same ideas that found such bold and logical expression in Price and others later, and were applied by them to the American situation, helping so much in that way to bring about the American Revolution. Price's own *Civil Liberty* had been read in France and had brought eminent Frenchmen into the list of his correspondents. The writers who acquired the greatest influence in this direction in France were Montesquieu, whose *Esprit des Lois* appeared in 1748 ; Voltaire ; and Jean-Jacques Rousseau, whose *Contrat Social*, published in 1762, provided more than any other work the philosophy of the French Revolution. The three Revolutions— English, American, and French—are thus essentially con- nected. The French Revolution was inspired primarily by a philosophy. For its occasion and immediate cause we have to look elsewhere, that is, to the quarrel between Crown and Parliament.

The bursting of the storm came with the fall of the Bastille, the State Prison, which the people regarded as the very emblem of tyranny and held in utter detestation. The historic date is July 14, 1789. It was Price's nephew, George Cadogan Morgan, who first transmitted to this country the news of the grim event. He was then in France, having gone thither on a holiday tour with three English friends. They had landed in Calais on July 4,

1789, and reached Paris on July 9. They were there taken
for spies and detained, but were allowed to leave the city
after the fall of the Bastille. On their way to the south
of France, where they continued their tour, they were
stopped by crowds inquiring for news from Paris.[1]
The news of the central act of the Revolution had a mixed
reception in England. Whig opinion generally was
strongly favourable to it. It was warmly welcomed
by the poets of the day, Wordsworth, Coleridge, Southey,
and Sheridan; by politicians, like Lord Lansdowne,
Lord Stanhope, Charles James Fox, and even William
Pitt; by lawyers, like Lord Erskine, one of the greatest
lawyers of the century; by men of science, like Joseph
Priestley; and by the Dissenters, who, almost to a man,
hailed the upheaval with the greatest delight. Price
welcomed it, and welcomed it with an unbounded enthusiasm. Many Welshmen shared the enthusiasm of
their fellow countryman, among them being ' Jac Glany-
gors ', ' Iolo Morgannwg '—the ' Bard of Liberty ', David
Williams, Morgan John Rhys, and Tomos Glyn Cothi.

The Revolution was regarded in Germany ' with glee '.
Immanuel Kant was loud in approval and praise. Gentz,
the political philosopher, whose attention ' no book or
pamphlet of importance published in France, England or
Germany escaped ', and who diligently ' studied Price
and Tom Paine ', recognized in the Revolution the ' first
practical triumph of philosophy '.[2]

When the news of the fall of the Bastille reached
England, Price was spending his accustomed holiday by
the sea, near Bridgend. So anxious was he to be nearer the
source of intelligence that he could hardly be prevailed

[1] Williams, *A Welsh Family*, p. 79.
[2] See Gooch, *Germany and the French Revolution*, chaps. ii–iv,
and *passim*.

upon to continue his stay in Wales. When, the holiday
over, he returned to London, he soon found himself at
the centre of the activities which the Revolution was
stirring in this country. He was, besides, in the favourable
position of being in constant communication with Thomas
Jefferson, then acting as ambassador of America in Paris,
and therefore well informed of the progress of events
there. George Cadogan Morgan was also in a position
to give his uncle first-hand information. He too, like
his uncle and his brother, William Morgan, was in touch
with Jefferson, corresponding and often dining with him.[1]
They were likewise in close touch with Franklin and Paine.

There had existed in England for nearly a century
a society known as the Revolution Society. Despite its
ominous name, it was nothing more, as its full title, ' The
Society for Commemorating the Revolution in Great
Britain', shows, than a Society to keep alive the memory of
the Revolution of 1688. Price's activities in relation to the
French Revolution are often directly associated with it,
and under its auspices.[2] It had met every year unin-
terruptedly for the whole period of its existence, on Nov. 4.
For many years its membership, drawn from among
Churchmen and Dissenters, was confined to London.
Latterly it had ' excited a more general attention, and
drawn to it many persons of rank and consequence from
different parts of the kingdom '. Among these were
members of the Peerage and of Parliament. When 1788,
the centenary of the Revolution, drew near, the Society

[1] Letter from Jefferson to Price, ' Paris, July 12, 1789 '. In *Price
Letters*.

[2] Almost every reference to the Society in this work is based upon
' An Abstract of the History and Proceedings of the Revolution
Society in London ; Published by Order of the Committee, 1789.'
In Dr. Williams's Library.

resolved to celebrate it in a special manner. The celebration took the form of a morning Sermon at the Old Jewry followed by an evening banquet at the London Tavern, presided over by Lord Stanhope. The importance of the occasion led the Committee to invite Price to deliver the Sermon. He declined, mainly on the ground of age and infirmity. But he attended, and took part in the proceedings. The Sermon was delivered by Dr. Kippis, there was an oration by Dr. Towers, and the character of King William, the hero of 1688, was read by Dr. Abraham Rees. The company was ' a numerous and respectable ' one of ' about 300 Gentlemen '. There was a list of forty-one toasts, opening with ' The Majesty of the People ', and closing with ' May Truth and Liberty prevail throughout the World '. Price proposed one of the toasts : ' The memory of the Bishops who were imprisoned in the Tower, and may all clerical men show themselves equal enemies to arbitrary power.' A business meeting held after the Dinner elected Price a member of the Committee for the ensuing year, his name appearing first on the list, which is not in alphabetical order. In the evening, the Monument was illuminated, and a transparent painting, emblematic of the glorious event, displayed in the front of the Tavern, containing the inscription, ' A Tyrant Deposed, And Liberty Restored, 1688 '. Here, indeed, the generous spirit of freemen glowed in every breast. All this was before the French Revolution broke out. That event, however, had burst upon the world before the next annual meeting of the Society came round on Nov. 4, 1789, and it invested the 1789 meeting with an importance and significance far surpassing even those of the centenary celebrations of the previous year. The extraordinary occasion once more pointed to Price as the one person to deliver the Sermon. Although he had a year before declined, he now felt himself compelled to accept the Committee's invitation. His glowing ardour made him forget his age and infirmity, and he undertook a task to the accomplishment of which his strength was not really equal. But his devotion to the cause of liberty so animated him that never did he serve that cause with greater effect than on that occasion, though he was in constant bodily pain and apprehensive lest he should fail to proceed with the service. It appears that he did not manage to go through the whole of what he had prepared, for the minutes speak of a ' part, which for want of time and strength, he did not deliver'. The Sermon was delivered in the Old Jewry, where Price, whose fame now extended to two continents, must have had crowding in upon him mixed memories of his early years there with Chandler. The Meeting-house was crowded to its utmost capacity. Price preached from the second and following verses of Psalm cxxii : ' Our feet shall stand within thy gates, O Jerusalem, whither the tribes go up ; the tribes of the Lord unto the testimony of Israel. To give thanks to the name of the Lord, for there sit the thrones of judgment, the throne of the House of David. Pray for the peace of Jerusalem. They shall prosper that love thee. Peace be within thy walls, and prosperity within thy palaces. For my brethren and companions' sake I will now say peace within thee. Because of the House of the Lord our God, I will seek thy good.' [1] From this text he delivered an eloquent and inspiring sermon on _The Love of Our Country_. The overflowing congregation could hardly be restrained by the sacredness of the place from bursting into shouts of applause. Price's Sermon was the first pronouncement of importance in

---

[1] The wording is as it appears at the head of the Sermon.

this country on the French Revolution, and from it dates
all discussion concerning the upheaval. ' The history of
the French Revolution in England begins with a sermon
and ends with a poem,' [1] the former, Price's *Love of Our
Country*, the latter Shelley's *Hellas*, separated by an
interval of thirty-two years. Truly has it been said that
it begins with ' the grave but enthusiastic prose of a
divine justly respected by earnest men ' ; it ends in
' the rapt vision, the magical music of a singer, who
seemed as he sang to soar beyond the range of human
ears '.[2]

The Sermon opens with a definition of 'our country', and
an account of the nature of our love to it. Love of country
is false when it is a contempt of other countries. It is
true when the passion is purified and made a ' rational
principle of action '.[3] We should love our country ' ardently but not exclusively ', and in pursuing its interest
we ' ought to carry our views beyond it '. We must
' consider ourselves as citizens of the world '.[4] The chief
blessings of a community are ' Truth, Virtue, and Liberty '.[5]
As to the first of these, Price lays great stress on our duty
to enlighten our country ; as to the second, he earnestly
wishes that all who profess zeal for their country's welfare
were ' as distinguished by the purity of their morals as
some of them are by their abilities '—' I cannot reconcile
myself ', he says, ' with the idea of an immoral patriot ; '
and as to the last, he insists that ' an enlightened and
virtuous country must be a free country '.[6] Magistrates
should be obeyed, but their authority, as also the authority
of kings, is to be understood as the authority of the
people entrusted to them.[7] A king is no more than the

---

[1] Brailsford, *Shelley, Godwin, and their Circle*, p. 7.   [2] Ibid.
[3] *Love of Our Country*, p. 7.   [4] Ibid., p. 10.
[5] Ibid., p. 11.   [6] Ibid., p. 19.   [7] Ibid., p. 24.

first servant of the community ' created by it, maintained by it, and responsible to it '. Therefore, ' his sacredness is the sacredness of the community ; his authority is the authority of the community ; and the term Majesty which it is usual to apply to him is by no means his own majesty, but the Majesty of the People.' [1] Price has here a very interesting example of the spirit in which Kings should always be addressed. Referring to the King's recovery from illness a short time previously he says that had he been to address the King on that occasion he would have been inclined to do it in a style very different from most of the addressers, and to use some such language as the following : ' I rejoice, Sir, in your recovery. I thank God for his goodness to you. I honour you not only as my King but as almost the only lawful King in the world, because the only one who owes his crown to the choice of his people. May you enjoy all possible happiness. May God show you the folly of those effusions of adulation which you are now receiving, and guard you against their effects. May you be led to such a just sense of the nature of your situation, and endowed with such wisdom as shall render your restoration to the government of these kingdoms a blessing to it, and engage you to consider yourself as more properly the Servant than the Sovereign of your people.' [2] Price, then sets forth the principles of the English Revolution and urges their importance : i. ' the right of conscience in religious matters ' ; ii. ' the right to resist power when abused ' ; and iii. ' the right to choose our own governors, to cashier them for misconduct, and to frame a government for ourselves '.[3] That Revolution brought Dissenters a measure of liberty

[1] *Love of Our Country*, pp. 23–4.
[2] Ibid., pp. 25–6.
[3] Ibid., p. 34.

in religion, and so was ' a great work ', but it was ' by
no means a perfect work ', as the existence of the Test
Laws, on the one hand, and the inequality of representation, on the other, show.[1] The peroration is a striking one,
eloquent with triumphant hope and joy : ' What an
eventful period is this ! I am thankful that I have lived
to see it ; and I could almost say, Lord, now lettest thou
Thy servant depart in peace, for mine eyes have seen Thy
salvation. I have lived to see a diffusion of knowledge
which has undermined superstition and error. I have
lived to see the rights of men better understood than
ever ; and nations panting for liberty which seemed to
have lost the idea of it. I have lived to see thirty millions
of people, indignant and resolute, spurning at slavery,
and demanding liberty with an irresistible voice ; their
king led in triumph, and an arbitrary monarch surrender-
ing himself to his subjects. After sharing in the benefits
of one Revolution, I have been spared to be a witness
of two other Revolutions, both glorious. And now,
methinks, I see the ardour for liberty catching and
spreading ; a general amendment beginning in human
affairs ; the dominion of kings changed for the dominion
of laws, and the dominion of priests giving way to the
dominion of reason and conscience. Be encouraged, all
ye friends of freedom, and writers in its defence ! The
times are auspicious. Your labours have not been in vain.
Behold kingdoms, admonished by you, starting from sleep,
breaking their fetters, and claiming justice from their
oppressors ! Behold the light you have struck out, after
setting America free, reflected to France, and there kindled
into a blaze that lays despotism in ashes, and warms and
illuminates Europe ! Tremble, all ye oppressors of the

[1] *Love of our Country*, pp. 25–42.

world! Take warning, all ye supporters of slavish governments, and slavish hierarchies! Call no more (absurdly
and wickedly) reformation, innovation. You cannot now
hold the world in darkness. Struggle no longer against
increasing light and liberality. Restore to mankind their
rights, and consent to the correction of abuses, before
they and you are destroyed together.' [1]

At the unanimous request of the Society the Sermon
was published. It was immediately read and admired
with a fervour hardly less than that with which it had
been listened to in the Old Jewry. Priestley declared that
it ' moved him to tears '.[2] The profound impression it
made may be summed up in a sentence in the words of
the Patriotic Society of L'Orient which speaks of ' Dr.
Price's Discourse ' as being ' one of the things that should
determine people to decide to lose life rather than cease
to be free '.[3] It ran quickly into several editions, was
translated into French, and drew forth a number of replies,
which, in turn drew forth other replies in its defence.
Price took no further part, beyond making a few explanatory remarks in a later edition of the Sermon, and issuing
in 1790 a ' Preface and Additions ' to it, neither of which
was controversial. 'Knowing,' he says, in the Preface to the
third edition, ' that it has been the labour of my life to
promote those interests of liberty, peace, and virtue . . .
and believing that I have not laboured quite in vain,
I feel a satisfaction that no opposition can take from me,
and shall submit myself in silence to the judgment of the
public.' To Price replied Burke, a pensioner of the
Government, with his *Reflections on the French Revolution*,
a work which, though a literary classic, is steeped in

---

[1] *Love of Our Country*, pp. 49-51.
[2] Lecky, *History of England in the Eighteenth Century*, vol. v,
p. 450.   [3] Letter to Revol. Soc., Aug. 8, 1790.

vituperative anger, and after the publication of which its author ' personally never recovered his place in the esteem of England '.[1] To Burke again replied Priestley, with his *Open Letters to Burke* ; James Mackintosh, with his *Vindiciae Gallicae*, which, however, he recanted later ; and Tom Paine, with his famous *Rights of Man*, which he began at the Angel Inn, Islington, where he was then staying, immediately upon the appearance of the *Reflections* in October or early in November.[2] For four years ' the mighty debate went on, and it became as the disputants conversed across the echoes of the Terror, rather a dialogue between the past and the future, than a discussion between human voices '.[3]

Later in the day on this same 4th of November, 1789, the Society held a Dinner followed by a business meeting in the London Tavern, and presided over by Lord Stanhope. The company was numerous, respectable, and in the highest spirits. At the Dinner Price moved a Congratulatory Address to the National Assembly of France. The measure of Price's ardour can be seen from the simple fact that immediately on his return home from the Old Jewry Service, and before coming to the Dinner, pain and fatigue completely overpowered him, and it was some hours before the utmost attention could afford him any relief. By the unanimous resolution of the meeting the Address was transmitted, with Price's speech, to the National Assembly. The full wording of the Address is ' The Society for commemorating the Revolution in Great Britain, disdaining national partialities, and rejoicing in every triumph of Liberty and Justice over Arbitrary Power, offer to the National Assembly of France their

[1] Conway, *The Life of Thomas Paine*, p. 118.
[2] Ibid., p. 113.
[3] Brailsford, *Shelley, Godwin, and their Circle*, p. 15.

Congratulations on the Revolution in that Country, and on the prospect it gives to the two first kingdoms in the World, of a common participation in the blessings of Civil and Religious Liberty. They cannot help adding their ardent wishes for a happy settlement of so important a Revolution, and at the same time expressing the particular satisfaction with which they reflect on the tendency of the glorious example given in France to encourage other Nations to assert the inalienable rights of Mankind, and thereby to introduce a general reformation in the Governments of Europe, and to make the world free and happy.' This Address was conveyed to the Duc de la Rochefoucauld in Paris with a letter requesting him to present it to the National Assembly. This he did, and he sent to the Revolution Society a copy of his speeches in the Assembly. The Archbishop of Aix, in his capacity of President, sent to the Society an extract from the votes of the Assembly for the 25th Nov. 1789, and signed by himself and the great Mirabeau as Secretary. The extract speaks of the ' loud applause ' with which the Address was received, and of the direction to the President to write to Stanhope expressing the ' lively and deep sensibility ' of the Assembly. Before the Archbishop sent the letter which he was thus directed to send to Stanhope, the Duc de la Rochefoucauld, not delaying ' to do *himself* the honour of writing to Dr. Price ', had sent to the latter a communication in which he refers to ' that great Apostle of Liberty, Dr. Price '. The Archbishop's letter containing his personal tribute as well as that of the Assembly, followed immediately.

These were by no means the only marks of approval received by Price and the Society. Price became the idol of all the French patriots who visited this country, and was constantly either meeting them or entertaining them at his own house, where his nephews, the brothers Morgan, met them often. Communications were received from all parts of France, mainly from the ' Patriotic Societies ' associated under the title of ' The Friends of the Constitution ', which had been established throughout that country, and were still multiplying there. Among these were those from Aix, Alais, Amiens, Auxerre, Arras, Brest, Bordeaux, Bayonne, Calais, Chalon-sur-Mer, Cresy, Cherbourg, Clermond-Ferrand, Cognac, Dijon, Grenoble, Hieres, Havre, Langon, Lisieux, Limoges, Lille, La Rochelle, L'Orient, Marseilles, Marrenes, Montargis, Montpelier, Nismes, Nantes, Paris (Young Friends), Pontoise, Rouen, Rennes, Saintes, St. Servan, Strasbourg, Toulouse (Young Friends), Tours, Versailles, Valence, and Vire. Apart from their expressions, which we will touch upon later, of a passionate respect for Price and of unbounded admiration for his work in the cause of liberty, these communications show two things quite clearly : that Britain was regarded in France as the pioneer in this struggle for liberty, and that it was a philosophy which was behind the Revolutions in England, America, and France, alike. To quote only an example or two : ' Why should we be ashamed ', asks the Society of Dijon, ' to acknowledge that the Revolution which is now establishing itself in our country is owing to the example given by England a century ago ? ' [1] ' It is to you, generous and brave English ! ' declares the Society of Saintes, ' it is to you that it belongs to propagate those great and immortal truths wrote in bright characters on the first page of the Code of Nature.' [2] The Society of La Rochelle speaks of the English and the French as the two people who will ' carry

[1] Extract from the Register.
[2] Letter, ' 9 June, 1791, and the Second Year of Liberty '.

THE CONSTITUTIONAL SOCIETY 133

the torch of Philosophy to the Regions which Despotism and Superstition still cover with their thick darkness '.[1] The Society of Toulouse, likewise, speaks of ' Liberty, which in its progress to-day, follows reason and philosophy '.[2]

Societies in this country, too, expressed their warm approval of Price. For the most part they were ' Constitutional ' Societies, such as those of Cambridge, Manchester, Norwich, and Taunton. Some of these became related to the Revolution Society as ' corresponding ' societies. The Constitutional Society—its full title was ' The Society for Promoting Constitutional Information '—of which these were constituent societies, was a much younger Society than the Revolution Society, for it only came into being in 1780, with the object of prosecuting the cause of Parliamentary Reform. It was established by Major Cartwright, whose toast as ' Father of the Society ' was proposed at its semi-annual Dinner mentioned below. Like the Revolution Society, it, too, was a very respectable body, with Dukes, Earls, and other people of rank rubbing shoulders with Tom Paine, whose *Rights of Man* it adopted as its Magna Carta.[3] Price was greatly interested in this Society also.

The Constitutional Society met at the London Tavern for its semi-annual Dinner on Dec. 16—a few weeks after the Revolution Society Dinner had been held there. Price was present. The list of twenty-six toasts opened with ' The Majesty of the People '. One of the toasts we must take special note of. It was ' Dr. Price, the Friend of the Universe '.[4] Price had left the room when it was

---

[1] Letter, ' October 2, 1790 '.
[2] Letter, ' 1 June, 1791, Year 2 of Liberty '.
[3] Conway, *Life of Thomas Paine*, p. 117.
[4] See *Gentleman's Magazine* for 1789, vol. lix, part 2, pp. 1183–4, for full account.

proposed, but, before leaving, he had communicated to the gathering the letter received by him from the Duc de la Rochefoucauld, mentioned above. The animation of the company must have been indeed great, when, in their just glorification of the work of the subject of their toast, they listened to the warm and eager tribute of Rochefoucauld to him as the ' great Apostle of Liberty '—a title by which he deserves to be for ever known.

July 14, 1790, was the first anniversary of the fall of the Bastille. The day was the occasion of further rejoicing on the part of the friends of Liberty in England, a Commemoration Dinner being held in the Crown and Anchor Tavern in the Strand. Price was foremost in this celebration again. Not only was he, as he himself tells us, concerned ' in calling together ' the friends of the Revolution ' to testify on that day their joy ', but he also proposed a toast. The company was by no means identical with that at one of the annual celebrations of the Revolution Society. Price says that it contained but ' an inconsiderable part ' of that Society's gathering at the feast of the previous Nov. 4, and ' it is probable ', he adds, ' that they will make but an inconsiderable part of the company that will attend our annual feast on the 4th of November next '. Though not identical with either of the two Societies which we have already noted, this gathering was that of a definite Society, for Price refers to it as ' this Society ', and of the ' Society ' as ' increasing ' though having ' no fixed President '. A new Society had come into existence for the commemoration of the French Revolution. The meeting, which was a ' very animating ' one of ' a very respectable company consisting of several hundreds of Gentlemen ', was presided over by Lord Stanhope. The toast which Price gave was ' An Alliance between France and Great Britain, for perpetua-

ting peace, and making the world happy '. His Address
was a high-toned expression of joy that the ' glorious
Revolution ' which they were celebrating promised ' a
new and better order in human affairs ', and of hope that
to prevent wars France and Great Britain would unite
and ' soon draw into their confederation ' the other
countries of Europe, so that when alarms of war came
they would be able to say to contending nations, ' Peace ',
and there would be Peace.[1] This Address, received with
enthusiastic applause, was, together with a resolution
proposed by Sheridan ' expressive of the joy of the company in the extension of liberty to France ', transmitted
through the Duc de la Rochefoucauld to the National
Assembly. Such was that body's approval of Price's
sentiments that every member thereof stood, and remained
standing, uncovered, while the Address was being read
a second time. Price tells us that this Dinner was con-
fused by some societies in France with that of the previous
November, that is with that of Nov. 4, 1789 ; and this
is obvious from the frequent references to this Address in
the communications to the Revolution Society, which
Society had nothing to do with this Dinner.

On Nov. 4, 1790, four months after the July Dinner
just mentioned, Price, though now in failing health,
was once more present at the anniversary meeting and
Dinner of the Revolution Society at the London Tavern.
In the absence of Lord Stanhope it was he who presided
over ' a very numerous ' gathering. In accordance with
a resolution to establish corresponding Societies throughout the country, which had been passed at the business
meeting after the Dinner twelve months before, it was

---

[1] Appendix to the *Preface and Additions to the Discourse on the
Love of Our Country.*

now reported that ' several Societies have been formed, and others are forming ' on the plan recommended. At this Dinner Price gave a toast, ' The Parliament of Britain —May it become a National Assembly '.[1] He had prepared an introduction to the toast and an explanation of it, but these he was not able to deliver. In consequence of misrepresentation of the toast, however, they were published. From them it is abundantly evident that Price meant no more by his toast than to express wishes of such a reform in the representation of the Kingdom as that Parliament might be justly deemed a *National* Assembly, or an Assembly truly representing the nation and speaking with its voice. A letter he had written only three weeks previously contains a note expressing the same view of what he regarded the Government of this country ought to be. There, having spoken of the French National Assembly, he says : ' The Government of Britain would be *nearly* such a government as is here meant, and its constitution *all* that the writer of this letter can wish to see it, were the three States that compose it perfectly independent of one another, and the House of Commons in particular, an equal and fair representation of the Kingdom, guarded against corruption by being frequently renewed, and the exclusion of placemen and pensioners.' [2]

This Dinner was Price's last public appearance on behalf of Liberty, the cause to which he had devoted his best talents and energies for so much of his life.

[1] Appendix to the *Preface and Additions to the Discourse on the Love of Our Country.*

[2] Letter, ' Oct. 14, 1790 ', from Price through Rochefoucauld to the inhabitants of the district of Quimper. Cf. a passage in *The Evidence for a Future Period of Improvement in the State of Mankind*, 1766, quoted above, p. 111.

CHAPTER IX

Price's failing strength — illness — sympathy of all classes — death —Kippis officiates at the funeral in Bunhill Fields—Priestley delivers the funeral sermon in the Gravel Pit — news of the death received with universal sorrow — Dinner to celebrate French Revolution — Toast to the Memory of Price, 'The Apostle of Liberty, and the Friend of Mankind' — Constitutional Dinner in Birmingham — The Memory of Price again toasted — expressions of sorrow and tributes from France.

BETWEEN the last two Dinners, that is, in the late summer of 1790, Price had spent two months by the sea near Newton, Bridgend. He had intended employing his leisure hours there in writing some memoirs of his own life, with a view to prefixing them to an additional volume of Sermons which he had meant to publish. But though he stayed longer than usual in Glamorgan he appears to have made no further progress in that work than to write an 'imperfect sketch' of the more important events of his later years. When he returned to London in October he lamented his 'growing infirmities' and 'total unfitness for any work that required either time or attention'. Nevertheless, as we have seen, he attended and presided over the Dinner early in November. During the winter he became more and more indisposed to engage in any literary work, with the consequence that he did not write the intended account of his life. The last of his literary labours was the preparation of a fourth edition of his treatise on *Reversionary Payments*, in two volumes. His progress in it was slow, and before the first volume was printed off he entrusted the work to his nephew, William Morgan, for completion. Price was still able, however, to discharge his duties as a Minister at the Gravel Pit, Hackney, with little or no interruption. Early in February, 1791, he officiated at a funeral in Bunhill Fields, and on his return home complained of having had to stand a considerable time in the open in inclement weather, remarking that that method of conducting funerals was a ' sure way of sending the living after the dead '. In the course of a month he attended another funeral, which was the means of his catching a chill, resulting in his being taken ill of a fever on Wednesday in the week following. He preached as usual on the intervening Sunday, February 20. The fever did not prove fatal, but it was a contributory cause of another malady which did. His illness had continued for about two months when a visible alteration for the worse took place. ' From the commencement of his illness ', we are told, ' his door was surrounded with anxious inquirers after his health ; in which were included the learned, the good, and the great of all persuasions.' [1] On Tuesday, April 19, ' a few minutes before three o'clock in the morning, having looked upon his nephew ', William Morgan, who attended him, and with his faculties still entire, ' he drew some short aspirations and quietly breathed his last '.[2] So passed away Richard Price. He was buried at one o'clock on Tuesday, April 26, in Bunhill Fields, in the same grave as his wife and his uncle, the tomb standing ' E. and W. 45, and N. S. 1 '.[3] He had expressed a wish that his funeral should be as private as possible, and his two nephews, William and George Cadogan Morgan, upon whom the arrangements devolved, had every intention of carrying out the wish. The former

[1] *Gentleman's Magazine*, for 1791, part 2, p. 673.

[2] Morgan, *Memoirs*, p. 177.

[3] *Bunhill Memorials*, pp. 216, 220.

tells us with regret, however, that they suffered their
better judgement to be overpowered by the solicitations
of their late uncle's friends and admirers, who prevailed
upon them to have the time of the funeral fixed for the
day instead of the night as they had at first intended.
But the further design of these friends to proceed ' through
some of the most public streets in London ' was ' peremp-
torily resisted ' and not carried out.[1] The hearse bearing
the remains ' was followed by twenty mourning coaches of
his family and immediate friends ' ; after which ' followed
a train of thirty gentlemen's carriages ', among them being
those of the Duke of Portland, Earl Stanhope, Rev.
Theophilus Lindsey, Rev. Thomas Belsham, and Mr.
Thomas Rogers, and a number of Members of Parliament
and persons of distinction.[2] The pall was supported by
' the Rev. Hugh Worthington, Rev. Samuel Palmer,
Rev. Thomas Tayler, Rev. R. Harris, D.D., Rev. A. Rees,
D.D., and Rev. Joseph Priestley, LL.D.' [3] The funeral
discourse was delivered by the Rev. Dr. Kippis, but
from the weakness of his voice he was very imperfectly
heard by the large concourse of people. Those who did
hear him were inspired with ' the veneration and respect
inseparable from the character of a great and good man '.[4]
On the following Sunday, May 1, the Rev. Dr. Priestley
delivered a funeral sermon in the Meeting-house of his
departed friend at the Gravel Pit, Hackney. It was
Priestley who succeeded to the pastorate there towards
the close of the same year. Both Kippis's and Priestley's
sermons were published. Price, who had no children,
' gave his residue in equal shares to his nephews William
Morgan and George Cadogan Morgan, and appointed them

---

[1] Morgan, *Memoirs*, pp. 179–80.
[2] *Gentleman's Magazine* for 1791, vol. lxi, part i, pp. 390, 486.
[3] Ibid.   [4] Ibid.

his executors ', by his Will bearing date ' the 25th of May,
1789 '.[1]

The news of Price's death was received with profound
sorrow in France as also it was received here and in
America. His memory was toasted at a Dinner held at
the Crown and Anchor Tavern, on July 14, 1791, to celebrate the second anniversary of the French Revolution.
There were present fifteen hundred gentlemen, among
whom were a great many, including Doctors Kippis,
Towers, and Rees, who had been Price's intimate friends.
George Rous was called to preside over the gathering,
Lord Stanhope, in consequence of the advice of his friends,
not being present. The fact that the meeting was under
observation did not deter the company from courageously
going through a list of twenty-one toasts, every one of
which offered a challenge to the old order and a passionate
welcome to the new. The list was headed by ' The Rights
of Man ', and included ' To the Memory of Dr. Price, the
Apostle of Liberty, and the Friend of Mankind ', which was
received with peculiar admiration and warmth at this the
first gathering commemorative of the Revolution since his
death. Besides, there was an additional tribute to Price paid
by one of the company, M. Couédic, a Breton, who had formerly been member of a French Parliament, possessed the
title of Marquis, and encountered much personal danger
by his struggles for liberty previous to the outbreak of
the Revolution. ' Gentlemen,' said he, ' Dr. Price, whose
excellent morals were expanded through the two worlds, is
no more among us, except in a remembrance, which will be
transmitted to future generations for the immortality of

---

[1] Memorandum by Mr. Walter Ashburner, great-grandson of
George Cadogan Morgan, and so a direct descendant of Price's
sister, into whose hands the greater part of the Price papers eventually
went. In *Price Letters*, Introd.

his name. If I repeat here the name of one of our patrons, and one of the fathers of civil and religious tolerance, it is because the name of Price is inseparable from the idea of peace and universal liberty, for he has left their rules in his profound and celebrated writings, and their seeds in his social and private virtues.' The company, at the Chairman's suggestion that they should retire early and quietly to their homes, then dispersed cheerfully and peaceably. A similar festive gathering held in Birmingham, mentioned here because Price's memory was enthusiastically toasted by those who attended it, among whom Priestley, like Stanhope in the London gathering, was not present, did not, however, pass unattended by dreadful consequences. At that Dinner,[1] a 'Constitutional' Dinner, held on the same day, July 14, 1791—one that became notorious as being the occasion and the immediate cause of the riot and disgraceful attack on Joseph Priestley's house, and the complete destruction by fire and otherwise of all that great scientist's manuscripts, leading to his quitting that town for London, and, after three years there, his making his home for the remainder of his life in America, already for him the asylum which Price foretold it would become—at this Dinner, one of the eighteen toasts was, ' To the Memory of Dr. Price, and of those illustrious sages who have enlightened mankind on the true principles of Civil Society '. But it is the unanimous expression of sorrow and the warm tributes to Price's memory which came from France which deserve special notice here. They indicate unmistakably how far-reaching Price's influence in France had been, and how deeply they felt the loss which his death had brought to them, and, indeed, to mankind. The Patriotic Society of Clermont-

---

[1] *Gentleman's Magazine*, 1791, vol. lxi, part 2, pp. 596–9, 675.

Ferrand tells the Revolution Society, ' The sorrow which
the death of the great Price brings us has re-opened in
our hearts the wound which the death of Mirabeau
made '.[1] The Society of Toulouse groups together ' Ly-
curgue, Solon, Franklin, Mirabeau, Price ' [2] as those for
whom it mourns. The Paris Society of the Friends of the
Constitution affirm that ' he had no other object than the
welfare of humanity ', and that by his devotion to
Liberty he ' sought neither vain honours nor dangerous
power ; he disdained the one and had refused the other '.
' Price ', it continues, ' merited, then, the title of benefactor
of mankind ; he was that especially to the French People,
since the Revolution in the United States had so much
influence on ours. He was interested only in the regenera-
tion of France, and he associated that with the regenera-
tion of all other nations. May he have many followers
in all Nations ! ' [3] The same letter informs the Revolution
Society that ' The Society of the Friends of the Constitution, Paris, has decided to wear mourning for this so justly
celebrated man. It is at once the mark of its particular
respect for this Friend of Man and of Liberty, and the
proof of the community of sentiment which it desires to
hold with your Society.' In an undated reply to this letter,
Benjamin Cooper, the Secretary of the Revolution Society,
assures his admirers that ' Doctor Price . . . was an
ornament to our Country and to human nature '. He
sought the establishment of its honour and prosperity
' not in the degradation of human nature by the enslave-
ment of his fellow creatures, but by the exertion of those
generous principles of Liberty which exalt and dignify the

[1] ' 2 May, 1791.' Mirabeau had died on the 2nd of April, a little
more than a fortnight before Price.
[2] ' 17 May, 1791.'
[3] ' 9 May, 1791.' The translation is ours.

social state '.   The minutes of the Society for May 11,
1791, speak of ' that Friend of Man, the late wise, learned,
and truly patriotic—Doctor Price '.   The Society of
Nantes writes, ' Price is dead, and all France has shed
tears for this implacable enemy of Tyrants, for this large-
hearted defender of Liberty ', and speaks of ' Doctor
Price, the Apostle of humanity, the honour and the glory
of a rival but generous Nation '.   ' Price and Mirabeau have
ceased to be, but their sensitive and burning souls are
now re-united in the bosom of the Deity.' [1]   The Friends
of the Constitution again pay tribute to ' the learned and
virtuous Price.' [2]   A reply to this letter testifies that
' Dr. Price was indeed a Great and Good Man . . . though
indefatigable in the pursuit of every object that could
be beneficial to Mankind, he conceived his labours crowned,
and his toil in a manner recompensed, in finding that the
sacred Flame of Liberty, which he himself had ever
cherished in his bosom, had not been entirely lost ; but
that in both this and the other Hemisphere it had sprung
with renovated ardour, and that its genial warmth still
promised to be more extensively and widely diffused ' ;
and that ' though more immediately a Citizen of England,
he was no less interested for the civil and religious Liberty
of the whole World, and for the happiness and welfare
of Human Nature '.[3]   The Patriotic Society of Bordeaux
writes, ' We have learnt with pain of the loss which you
have suffered by the death of Dr. Price.   We have put on
mourning for him as we did for Franklin and Mirabeau.'
' Dr. Price, like the two great men who predeceased him,
extended his vision over the whole of mankind.   Religious
and Civil Liberty, Universal Liberty, had been the objects

[1] ' 12 May, 1791.'   The translation is ours.
[2] ' 21 May, 1791, and the Second Year of French Liberty.'
[3] ' 16 November, 1791.'

of his desires and of his labours, and like them he carried
with him to the grave the Consolation of having seen the
Dawn of a better Century, and of having spread some rays
of light on its Horizon.' [1]   The Society of Toulouse sends a
second letter asking ' Who better deserves to be called the
benefactor of mankind than he ? ' applying to him the
title ' Apostle of Liberty ', which Rochefoucauld and the
National Assembly had accorded him, and saying that
it has ' put on mourning for this Friend of humanity ',
and further that it has ' devoted two special sittings to
make known his Virtues '.[2]   ' Gentlemen,' says a reply
from the Revolution Society, ' it is not for us to dispute
your interest in him, whom you make your own by a
congeniality of sentiment, but rather to glory that our
Country has produced a Man so worthy of your applause.
Yes, the principles of Doctor Price are the property of
the whole Universe.' [3]   The communication of the Society
of Saintes deserves to be quoted almost in full : ' O !
Price ! worthy friend of Man and of the French !   You
the honour of Albion, and the Pride of Mankind !   You
we have lamented as a brother and a fellow-citizen, what
is become of this generous and lofty genius which draws
so boldly the picture of our Revolution ?   Death, dreadful
death, has frozen this burning soul, inexhaustible source
of brightness and virtue.   What do I say, my Brothers ?
Price has not ceased to live, he respires among you ;
he inspires your heart, as the soul of the great Mirabeau,
always in the possession of the Tribune . . . Breathe on
our august Legislators this wit of order and wisdom
which can never forsake them.   Price !   Mirabeau !
immortal names, become a sign for rallying all the real

[1] ' 21 May, 1791.' The translation is ours.
[2] ' 1 June, 1791, and the Year 2 of Liberty.' The translation is ours.
[3] ' Nov. 16, 1791.'

Patriots, and friends of the truth! May your celestial
influence fix for ever true principles in the Patriotic
Societies! May it shine in their deliberations, and rule
their actions of the least consequence. Be our tutelar
Gods, watch on the two Nations . . .'[1] The Society of
Nismes tells the Revolution Society, ' You have suffered
an irreparable loss in the person of Doctor Price; that
great man ceased not to honour his Nation in showing the
Universe to what height the human mind can rise, when,
with a pure heart, it engages itself to know the impre-
scriptible Rights of Man '; and describes Price as the
' torch of Liberty '.[2] The Society of Limoges states in
a postscript, ' We have taken mourning for your com-
patriot, the illustrious Doctor Price '.[3] ' Hardly had
our tribunes left off singing the funeral praises of the
immortal Mirabeau ', says the Society of Aix, when
' a fresh cry of pain makes itself heard! Death has just
struck also the fiery Orator, who, in the midst of a free
People, pleaded like him the cause of the People oppressed
by Tyranny! Doctor Price is no more! This Apostle
of Liberty . . . was the friend of Mankind . . . He dared to
show that proud titles, based on the accident of birth,
and proud wealth, should not give to a small number of
men in each Nation the exclusive right of ruling at their
will. He proved that it is to virtue and merit recognized
by all and chosen by the greatest number, and to them
alone, belongs the right to govern and administer the
People according to Laws which they themselves have
imposed.' The Society also decided to ' wear mourning
for Doctor Price ', and to ' have recorded in its Registers
the testimony of the pain it felt on learning of the death

[1] ' 9 June, 1791, and the Second Year of Liberty.'
[2] ' 11 June, the Second Year of Liberty.' The translation is ours.
[3] ' 14 June, 1791.'

of this eloquent and zealous defender of oppressed
Peoples '.[1]

Not only did ' three millions ' of the citizens of France
go into mourning for him,[2] but the National Assembly
itself ' went into mourning for six days for him ',[3] and
the Patriotic Society of Nantes resolved to place a bust
of him in their Hall by the side of the ' Declaration of the
Rights of Man ', and also to name a part of their town
' Le Quartier de Richard Price '.[4]

[1] ' 27 June, 1791.' The translation is ours.
[2] MS. History of Hackney, quoted by Prosser in *Historical Sketches
of Glamorgan*.
[3] Williams, *A Welsh Family*, p. 93.
[4] MS. History of Hackney, quoted by Prosser, ibid.

CHAPTER X

The Man : person — constitution — fondness for exercise — large heart and massive intellect — benevolent disposition — shown towards the mute creation, his own people, children, his country, and mankind — immensely popular and lovable — humility and candour — faithfulness to his calling as Minister of the Gospel — fervour and constancy in prayer — spiritual atmosphere — summary characterization.

WE turn now to note some of the features of Price's character and private life. Much of our information is what Samuel Rogers, the poet, has handed down. Price and Thomas Rogers, the poet's father, were not only very near neighbours, but, as we have seen, very intimate friends, holding the same political opinions and religious beliefs. For these reasons, and because also the Rogers family were members of Price's congregation at Newington Green, they would have special opportunities of knowing Price.

Price, Rogers tells us, was ' slim in person, and rather below the common size, but possessed of great muscular strength and remarkable activity. With strong features, and a very intelligent eye, his countenance was the mirror of his mind ; and when lighted up by conversation his features were peculiarly pleasing.' [1] The story of how a portrait of him was taken is interesting. His friends

[1] Williams, *A Welsh Family*, p. 17. The portrait of him reproduced by permission in this volume is from an engraving by Holloway, after West, whose original painting of him is now in the possession of the Royal Society, to whom it was presented by Arthur Morgan.

tried in vain to persuade him to have it taken. Price injured himself slightly by a fall from his horse. The doctor who attended him and whose care Price appreciated very highly, asked as his reward that his patient should sit for his painting. Price could do no other than consent. The painting was accordingly made by Benjamin West, who succeeded Joshua Reynolds in the Presidency of the Royal Academy.

Price never enjoyed a strong constitution, but by a simple and regular life, attention to moderate exercise, and the cultivation of a serene and equable temper, he kept himself in good if not robust health. He rode a great deal. Riding was, of course, much more common in those days than it is in ours. But he was particularly fond of that form of exercise. In this respect he resembled his friend the Marquis of Lansdowne, who was in the habit of riding ' from thirty to forty miles a day '. Price had had splendid opportunities for riding when, as a boy, he spent his vacations at Tynton, where the stables were well provided, and never without at least one white horse—a little fact which explains a partiality in Price, for, as we have seen, it was on a white horse that he always rode through the streets of London. Another favourite recreation of his was swimming, which he indulged in regularly. We are told that it was Price's ' custom every day at two o'clock to run off for a swim to Pearless Pool ' ; [1] and he delighted in every opportunity to bathe in the sea at Southerndown in his native Glamorgan. A few amusing stories illustrate in their way what athletic capacity he possessed. He once challenged ' a much taller and more robust person than himself to hop the length of the first field ' near the Meeting-

---

[1] Clayden, *Early Life of Samuel Rogers*, p. 9.

house at Stoke Newington, and won the race. On
another occasion, he attempted to leap over a honey-
suckle bush in the grass plot in the Rogers's garden, but
' strangled the tree between his legs, and away went the
honey-suckle and the doctor together '. The story was
going the round among Samuel Rogers's playmates that
the philosopher ' had once leaped over the new river.' [1]

The medium frame carried a large heart and a massive
intellect. It is difficult to know for which of these Price
remains most distinguished. His mental power was
evident in all he did. He was a rare intellectual genius.
Of this his published writings are an ample testimony.
His thinking was marked by great acuteness, strength,
and originality. ' No less a man than Condorcet ', we
are reminded, ' refers to him as one of the formative minds
of the century.' [2] His largeness of heart was no less
evident throughout his life, and not least even in his
writings. Goodness was the soul of all his work. His life
was the embodiment of the best elements in his own
teaching ; his writings were the true expression of his
life. ' It was not mere mental ability ', says his friend
Priestley, ' that could enable a man to write like him ;
it required perfect integrity as well as a sound understanding.' [3] The two qualities went together perfectly
in him. More than once do we find him referred to as
' the great and good Dr. Price '. ' Europe ', says Belsham,
' may be traversed in vain in search of an abler head or
a better heart.' [4] Hence the unique influence and power
of all his works, of all of which ' there was scarcely one
that did not exhibit qualities rarely found '.[5]

---

[1] Ibid.   [2] Brailsford, *Shelley, Godwin, and their Circle*, p. 11.
[3] *A Discourse on the occasion of the death of Dr. Price.*
[4] *Essays*, vol. i, p. 478.
[5] Doran, *Last Journals of Horace Walpole*, vol. i, p. 529 n.

Price's benevolent disposition manifested itself on the lowest levels as on the highest. He bore almost the love of a St. Francis for the mute creation. Here, again, a few anecdotes, though trivial enough in themselves, are interesting. ' In his field near his house he once saw some larks struggling in the nets in which they had just been caught. He cut the nets and set them free, but ' —such was his conscientiousness—' reflecting on the loss he had thereby caused to some unknown person, returned and deposited some money on the spot.' Similarly while on one of his walks, ' he suddenly remembered that he had seen a beetle on its back, and he returned through several fields, found it, and set it on its legs '. The absent-mindedness he betrayed here arose from the serious thought in which he was wont to indulge on his walks and at other times ; he once went down ' to his study to supper an hour after he had taken the meal '.[1]

Price's sympathy for the mute creation was but the manifestation on a lower level of that feeling for all sentient beings which found noble expression on the higher level of the love of mankind. Price's love for his fellow-beings knew no bounds. He loved his own. He loved his country. He loved mankind.

Price loved his own passionately. His crossing many miles of mountains and winter snows to see his mother, his sharing his meagre inheritance between her and his sisters, his forwarding to the latter the small sum of money which his diligence and success at the Moorfields Academy had brought him, all show how fully and joyfully, even in his tender years, he could sacrifice himself in love for those who were near to him. And we see him the same in his later years. His invalid wife found almost her only

[1] Clayden, *The Early Life of Samuel Rogers*, pp. 9–10.

enjoyment in playing cards. He himself found no enjoyment in that pastime in itself; he considered time spent
at it as wasted. Nevertheless, so much did he forget his
own self that to entertain her he would sit down every
evening to a card table and play until late with a cheerfulness and good humour which charmed everybody. It
was in the family circle, in fact, that his delightful qualities
were most conspicuous. Rogers, who was so often
privileged to be within the circle, assures us that ' there
it was that his character shone with the fullest lustre '.[1]
It was with the utmost sincerity and truth that William
Morgan could say of his mother and sister when they
went up to keep house for Price that they had ' the best
man in the world to live with '.

Having no children of his own, Price took great interest
in the children of the neighbourhood. He was as great
a favourite with them as he was with their parents. They
enjoyed his sympathy ' in their lessons and even in their
games '. Sometimes he would take them to his house to
show them how some of the scientific instruments, such
as the microscope and the telescope, which he had there,
worked. Between him and his young relatives, nephews
and nieces, also, there was the sincerest attachment. The
time he spent in their company when on his visits to South
Wales he thoroughly enjoyed. Margaret, the only daughter
of his brother John, was an especial favourite with him—
so completely had he put out of his thoughts the measured
kindness of his brother when he turned to him for help
in his orphan years.[2]

[1] Williams, *A Welsh Family*, p. 46.

[2] It is worth noting some later history connected with this
favourite niece. She married ' Mr. Lewis, of Newhouse, a very pretty
place near Cardiff ', not very far from Park where she lived with her
father. Her brother Samuel Price—John Price's eldest son—had no

He loved his country, too—'ardently, but not exclusively'. He was a true patriot. He never feared to point out his country's wrongs, nor did he ever fail to rejoice in its good. His patriotism was not in the remotest degree selfish or self-seeking. Sir William Jones speaks of him as one of those 'who love their country better than their interest'.[1] Priestley testifies to the same effect: 'His patriotism, though warm, was ever of the purest kind, looking to nothing for himself; and when he had the freest access to men in power, never using it for his own emoluments or that of his nearest friends. In this situation he conferred favours, but never received any.'[2] The wider patriotism, however, did not exclude the narrower. Price remained always deeply attached to Wales, the country of his birth. He paid regular visits to it, and invariably derived therefrom refreshment of body and soul. He was proud of the vote he possessed and exercised for his native Glamorgan. He was fond of extolling the beauties of Wales to his friends in the metropolis. A little incident reminds us how well, too, he thought of its inhabitants, his fellow-countrymen. Commenting upon his strong and patriotic feeling, Rogers says that once when Price was riding towards Wales on one of his visits thither, accompanied, as he often was, by some English friends, a friend observed that 'there were very few gentlemen's seats in the country'; where-

children, so that it was to Margaret Lewis's descendants that the accumulated fortune of her grandfather, Rees Price, went. Her son, Wyndham Lewis, became M.P. for Cardiff, and died leaving a widow, who afterwards married Lord Beaconsfield. In this way the Tynton wealth 'added brilliancy to a great career'.

[1] Letter, 'Crishna—Nagur, Sept. 26, 1788'. In Morgan, *Memoirs*, p. 115.

[2] *Discourse on the death of Dr. Price.*

upon Price replied, ' Wait till to-morrow, and every house you will see will be a gentleman's.' [1]

With his love for kith and kin and countrymen went his love for mankind. Price ' extended his vision over the whole of mankind '.[2] All measures for the ameliora- tion of man had his heartiest support. He befriended John Howard, the prison reformer, with inspiration, encouragement, and help. He corresponded with him when Howard was visiting the lazarettos of Europe, and assisted him to write his book on Prisons : ' People are not aware ', Rogers reminds us, ' that Dr. Price wrote a portion of it.' [3] Not only so, but it is even probable that Howard's success may be traced to his life-long friend, Price, as its real source. ' I am ashamed ', Howard tells Price, ' how much I have accumulated your labour ; yet I glory in that assistance, to which I owe so much credit in the world, and, under Providence, success in my endeavours. It is from your kind aid and assistance, my dear friend, that I derive so much of my character and influence.' [4] Price contributed very liberally to good causes. Priestley says that Price's circumstances were by no means what the world would call affluent, considering that he lived near the metropolis, ' and in the society of the most opulent in it '. But his ' style of life was of the simplest kind, and he was rich, as almost any man may be, by his moderation and economy '. From a moderate income he had a considerable surplus, in the distribution of which he was most judicious and liberal. ' When, in my great intimacy with him, I

[1] Williams, *A Welsh Family*, p. 49.

[2] Communication, ' May 21, 1791 ', from the Patriotic Society of Bordeaux.

[3] Powell, *Reminiscences and Table Talk of Samuel Rogers*, p. 114.

[4] Stoughton, *Howard the Philanthropist and his Friends*, p. 273.

was some years ago demonstrating against one particular instance of his liberality,' says Priestley, ' he told me he made it a rule to spend one-fifth of his income in some form of charity, and only wished to produce the greatest good by it, but that, had he had children, he would have contented himself with giving a tenth.' [1] His work on Annuities was done with the one object of serving the community. It was this love of mankind that made him the foe of lawless ambition and usurped power. He kept a never-ceasing vigil over the Rights of Man. He was the ' Apostle of Liberty ' *because* he was the ' Friend of Mankind '. He himself, in the evening of his life, described it as ' a life devoted to inquiry, and spent in endeavours (weak indeed and feeble) to serve the best interests, present and future, of mankind '.[2]

Price enjoyed immense popularity. Bearers of messages were anxious to wait upon him in person and so secure the honour of an introduction. Rogers tells us of his once accompanying him ' with five or six young men who loved his society ' on the return from Brighton to London. When passing through Horsham ' a gentleman ran after them to solicit Dr. Price to return and sleep at his house that night '. It would confer the greatest favour on himself, the inquirer assured him, to have ' an evening spent with Dr. Price ' [3]—who, however, was unable to gratify the request. The varied interests which his writings and activities embraced, and the wide world in which he moved, brought him, also, the intimate friendship of many of the best men then living. His house was the meeting-place of the learned and the great. ' It would

[1] *Discourse on the death of Dr. Price*, p. 16.

[2] Preface to his pamphlet *Observations on the Importance of the American Revolution*.

[3] Williams, *A Welsh Family*, pp. 91–2.

be impossible ', says Kippis, ' to do justice to the number
and respectability of his friends ' ; they were ' of the
first distinction for rank and knowledge and virtue ',
and included those which stood ' the highest in the
records of science, of learning, of freedom, and of moral
worth '.[1] Many of them, like himself, won enduring
fame. They included : Benjamin Franklin, Thomas
Jefferson, Joseph Priestley, John Adams, Sir John Pringle,
President of the Royal Society, David Hume, Adam Smith,
Andrew Kippis, Jonathan Shipley, Bishop of St. Asaph,
Edmund Law, Bishop of Carlisle, John Douglas, Bishop of
Salisbury, William Adams, Master of Pembroke College,
Oxford, the Marquis of Condorcet, James Necker, Jacques
Turgot, Rabaut St. Etienne, Tom Paine, John Howard,
John Horne Tooke, Sir William Jones, Lord Erskine, Lord
Ashburton—the two greatest lawyers of the century—
Lord Lyttleton, the Marquis of Lansdowne, and Earl
Stanhope. There were few greater men than these in
their countries in their day. Dr. Johnson had no love for
Price. Johnson was present at Oxford, probably in the
house of Dr. Adams, Master of Pembroke College, who
was a mutual friend, when Price came into the company.
At the sight of him, Johnson ' instantly left the room '.[2]
Samuel Rogers carried letters of introduction from Price
to Adam Smith and others when he visited Scotland.[3]
In America and France Price was regarded with ' a
veneration and affection that cannot be expressed '.[4] His
correspondence, only a fragment of which remains, was
so extensive that he often complained of it as a burden.
It is the simple truth that ' Dr. Price had no enemies,

[1] *An Address at the interment of the Rev. Dr. Richard Price.*
[2] Boswell, *Life of Johnson*, Oxford ed., vol. ii, p. 508.
[3] Dyce, *Table Talk of Samuel Rogers*, p. 22.
[4] Kippis, *Address at the interment of the Rev. Dr. Richard Price.*

but such as were enemies to his public principles; and among those who differed the most from him in this respect, many were his zealous and affectionate admirers '.[1] The same testimony is borne by the remark that he was ' no one's enemy any farther than his character required it of him '.[2] It is not surprising that ' perhaps there never was a private person who received so many marks of public esteem '.[3] He was deeply revered by the friends of liberty throughout the world.

It was one of the marks of Price's greatness that with his popularity went the greatest humility and candour. Priestley says that he ' never knew a person less sensible of his own excellences or so little elated by the great celebrity to which he attained ', a celebrity ' greater than any dissenting minister ever acquired before him '—and we may add, has ever acquired since. It is this humility that shows itself in his candour. Price held firmly to his opinions, but he was an enemy to bigotry. He would admit an error with the utmost readiness when he was convinced of it, but would never sacrifice his opinions to complaisance. In public controversy his ingenuous good temper led him always to express his doubts in the frankest manner. He had the greatest respect for honest opinions, and even when he thought his own well-founded, he never thought the worse of those who differed from him. Candour was native to him. Price had no shadow of guile in him. ' To intrigue, to art, to concealment, he was a perfect stranger : he always looked and spoke what his feelings dictated.' [4] His humility, candour, and simplicity in society have been beautifully set forth by

[1] Kippis, *Address at the interment of the Rev. Dr. Richard Price.*
[2] *Gentleman's Magazine* for 1791, part 2, p. 389.
[3] Kippis, *Address at the interment of the Rev. Dr. Richard Price.*
[4] Ibid.

Mrs. Chapone, who portrays him as ' Simplicius ' in one of her essays : ' While the vain man is painfully striving to outshine all the company, and to attract their admiration by false wit, forced compliments, and studied graces, he must surely be mortified to observe how constantly Simplicius engages their attention, respect, and complacency, without having once thought of himself as a person of any consequence among them. Simplicius imparts his superior knowledge, when called upon, as easily and naturally, as he would tell you what it is o'clock ; and with the same readiness and goodwill informs the most ignorant or confers with the most learned. He is as willing to receive information as to give it, and to join the company as far as he is able, in the most trifling conversation into which they happen to fall, as in the most serious and sublime. If he disputes, it is with as much candour on the most important and interesting as on the most insignificant subjects, and he is not less patient in hearing him than in answering his antagonist. If you talk to him of himself or his works, he accepts praise or acknowledges defects with equal meekness, and it is impossible to suspect him of affectation in either. We are more obliged and gratified by the plain unexaggerated expressions of his regard, than by the compliments and attentions of the most accomplished pattern of high breeding ; because his benevolence and sincerity are so strongly marked in every look, word, and action, that we are convinced his activities are offered for our sakes, not for his own, and are the natural effects of real kindness, not the studied ornaments of behaviour. Every one is desirous of showing him kindness in return, which we know will be accepted just as it is meant. All are ready to pay him that deference which he does not desire, and to give him credit for far more than he assumes, or even for more than he possesses. With a person ungraceful, and with manners unpolished by the world, his behaviour is always proper, easy, and respectable ; as free from constraint and servility in the highest company, as from haughtiness and insolence in the lowest. His dignity arises from his humility ; and the sweetness, gentleness, and frankness of his manners, from the real goodness and rectitude of his heart, which lies open to inspection in all the fearlessness of truth, without any need of disguise or ornament.' [1] Similar testimony comes from others. The Duchess of Bedford once expressed to Lord Lansdowne a desire to meet Price. A meeting was arranged at Lansdowne House. The Duchess afterwards said that whereas she ' expected to meet a Colossus, with an eye like Mars to threaten and command ', she was greatly astonished to find him a man of ' quiet aspect and unassuming manners '. Gibbon, the historian, is reported to have expressed similar surprise when he met him in Cadell's shop.[2] Mrs. Chapone's description of Price's manners as ' unpolished by the world ', is but confirmed by Rogers's differently worded statement that ' his manners were extremely polished '. How both these apparently discrepant statements are true is shown by Priestley's testimony that a ' simplicity of manners ' and ' perfect integrity and benevolence ' ' diffused round him a charm which the forms of politeness can but poorly imitate ',[3] and by Rogers's further testimony to the ' sweetness of his disposition ' and the ' unaffected sincerity of his manners '—' it was the perfect simplicity and sincerity of his character which gave dignity to his appearance.' [4]

[1] Miscellanies, Essay I. In Chalmers, *British Essayists*, vol. xviii.
[2] Clayden, *Early Life of Samuel Rogers*, pp. 34–5.
[3] *A Discourse on the death of Dr. Price.*
[4] Williams, *A Welsh Family*, p. 17.

Price's society, Priestley says, ' was coveted by those who were bred in courts, as superior to anything they found in the most polished circles '.[1]   When engaged in conversation he ' turned his wig round on his temples, twisted one leg round the other, and folded his cocked hat into a thousand shapes ', his countenance was ' lighted up ', and his features were ' particularly pleasing '.[2]   ' He who can have and truly enjoy the society of such a man as Dr. Price ', says Priestley again, ' cannot envy the condition of princes.'   ' Such fellowship ', he assures us, ' is the true balsam of life ;   its cement is infinitely more durable than that of the friendships of the world, and it looks for its proper fruit and complete gratification to the life beyond the grave.' [3]

Price's calling, it must not be forgotten, was that of a Minister of the Gospel.   Preaching the Gospel was his life's work.   Nothing was allowed to interfere with that, or with his pastoral work.   He was greatly beloved of his people, and every reference to him in his pastoral capacity after the first few years—when he was so dejected that he thought of renouncing the Ministry—is a happy one. His religion may be described in his own words as ' not a sour or enthusiastical religion but a rational and liberal and catholic religion, a religion free from bigotry, superstition, and uncharitableness, and that shows itself in all good works and amiable qualities as well as in the discharge of the duties of devotion '.[4]   As a preacher Price had eloquence, if not oratory.   His delivery was unstudied, but it made the deeper impression in that it came from

---

[1]   *A Discourse on the death of Dr. Price.*

[2]   Clayden, *Early Life of Samuel Rogers,* p. 10.

[3]   Preface to ' *A Free Discussion* '.

[4]   Letter to his sister, Mrs. Morgan, June 17, 1770 ;   In Williams, *A Welsh Family,* pp. 28–9.

the heart. An incident related by Rogers shows how deep that impression could be. ' In my boyhood ', he says, ' my father one day called me and my brothers into his room, and asked us each what professions we wished to follow. When my turn came, I said (to my father's annoyance) that I should like to be a preacher ; for it was then the height of my ambition to figure in the pulpit—I thought there was nothing on earth so grand.' ' This predilection, I believe,' he states further, ' was occasioned chiefly by the admiration I felt for Dr. Price and for his preaching.'[1] Like his uncle, the co-pastor of Watts, Price was eminent for his gift in prayer. ' His devotions were accompanied with an humility and fervour that powerfully engaged every well-disposed heart.' ' The particular fervour of his devotion ever expressed in the most natural and unaffected manner,' Priestley reminds his hearers, ' you must have constantly observed in the pulpit, and in all his public services of which prayer made a part ; and the deep sense that he had of the constant presence and providence of God was always apparent in his conversation on religious subjects. But such marks of strong devotional feelings as he discovered when he was under less constraint, in the more private devotions of his family (of which some of his more familiar religious friends must have been occasionally witnesses) I have seldom seen in any other person . . . I can compare the earnest manner in which he always expressed himself at those times to nothing but what we may conceive to have been that of our Saviour in the garden, when, in prayer to his Almighty father he said, Not my will, but Thine be done. No doubt he felt more intensely still

[1] Dyce, *Table Talk of Samuel Rogers*, pp. 2–3.

in his more private devotions, when, with or without the use of words, he poured out his whole heart to his Father who seeth in secret. It was evident to all his acquaintance that his devotion was both intense and habitual, the idea of God and of his providence being never long absent from his mind.' [1] It may be truly said that Prayer was the natural expression of Price's personality. He believed in devoting ' the greater part of an hour every morning or evening ' to the duties of serious recollection, self-examination, and private prayer, besides ' more time on Sundays and at other extraordinary seasons ', and urged that there should run through the rest of the day ' prevailing piety and goodness and a spirit of love and humility ', that our prayers, that is, ' should be accompanied by a holy life '.[2] His prayerful attitude of soul created around him a deeply spiritual atmosphere as the natural atmosphere of his presence. ' He would often drop in, to spend the evening with us, in his dressing gown,' says Rogers ; ' he would talk and read the Bible to us till he sent us to bed in a frame of mind as heavenly as his own.' [3] ' No person well acquainted with Dr. Price ', Priestley asserts, ' could say that rational sentiments of Christianity are unfriendly to devotion.' [4] There is no doubt that it is to the holiness of the world within him that we are to look for an explanation of a large measure of Price's power and influence over the epoch-making events of the world without.

Price is briefly, but fittingly, characterized in the words of the inscription on the marble Tablet erected to his

[1] *A Discourse on the death of Dr. Price.*
[2] Price, *Dissertation on Prayer.*
[3] Dyce, *Table Talk of Samuel Rogers*, p. 3.
[4] *A Discourse on the death of Dr. Price.*

memory in Stoke Newington Chapel in 1841, during the pastorate of Thomas Cromwell. It reads :

To the Memory of Richard Price, D.D., F.R.S., Twenty-six years
Minister of this Chapel ; Born at Tynton, Glamorganshire,
February 23, 1723 ;
Died at Hackney, Middlesex, April 19, 1791.
Theologian, Philosopher, Mathematician ; friend to freedom as to
virtue ; brother of man ; lover of truth as of God ; his eminent
talents were matched by his integrity, simplicity, and goodness
of heart ; his moral dignity by his profound humility.
Few have been more useful in their generation, or more valued by
the wise and good ; none more pure and disinterested.
Honoured be his name ! Imitated his example !

Of Price it may be truly said that on the subjects and causes nearest his heart he wrote and spoke with burning zeal, and the energy of a Brutus, having the eye to see around him despotism swaying an iron sceptre over almost the whole earth, the ear to hear the cry of misery arising from the oppressed, and a heart to feel deeply their sufferings.

Throughout his life he had the merit of having, like the ancient prophet, and with the same holy fervour, cried aloud and spared not, and at its close he could with the purest satisfaction say, *Liberavi animam meam.*

NOTE ON THE WELSH DISSENTING ACADEMY UNDER THE REV. VAVASOR GRIFFITHS

THE WELSH DISSENTING ACADEMY

THE whole question of the history of the Academy best
known under the name of 'Llwynllwyd', one of the
places where it was held, is still undetermined. Three
places are involved: 'Llwynllwyd', a farm-house in
the parish of Llanigon, near Hay, in Breconshire, Hay
being, it should be remembered, a border town of three
counties, Breconshire, Herefordshire, and Radnorshire;
'Maesgwyn', another farm-house, which used to be
regarded as being situated in the immediate neighbourhood of Llwynllwyd, but which the Rev. T. Shankland has
distinctly shown [1] to be twenty-five miles away therefrom
and situated near the village of Bugeildy, near Knighton,
in Radnorshire; and 'Chancefield', a part of the town of
Talgarth, in Breconshire, and about four miles distant from
Llwynllwyd. Again, two tutors, or supposed tutors, are
involved: the Rev. Vavasor Griffiths, who lived at
Maesgwyn and ministered to the dissenting church of that
name in that locality; and the Rev. David Price, who
lived in Llwynllwyd and ministered at Maesyronnen, near
Glasbury, between Hay and Talgarth, but on the Radnorshire side of the river Wye.

That there was a school at Maesgwyn—by which is
not meant the school that existed at Maesgwyn before
the Academy was there, but that Academy itself—with
Vavasor Griffiths as its tutor, and a school at Llwynllwyd,
with David Price connected with it, are alike, now, matters

[1] *Y Beirniad*, Cyf. viii, Rhif i, Awst 1918.

of agreement among those who have investigated in these directions. It is also agreed that both Howell Harris and William Williams, of Pantycelyn, studied at Llwyn-llwyd. The problem ranges itself, on the one hand, around the tutorship of Vavasor Griffiths at Llwynllwyd ; and, on the other, around, probably, the dual question of the existence, and the tutorship, of a school at Chance-field.

i. As to the first of these—the question of the tutor-ship of Vavasor Griffiths at Llwynllwyd—the Rev. T. Shankland, M.A., the historian-librarian of the Univer-sity College, Bangor, in a Welsh article on ' Pwy oedd Athro Williams Pantycelyn yn Llwynllwyd ? ' (' Who was Williams Pantycelyn's Tutor at Llwynllwyd ? ') in the *Beirniad*, vol. viii, no. 1, August 1918, seeks to confine Vavasor Griffiths's tutorship to Maesgwyn. His argument, as the Rev. D. Edmondes Owen, in an article mentioned below, points out, may be said, briefly, to consist of two parts : firstly, that since Maesgwyn and Llwynllwyd were twenty-five miles apart—a fact which the article has done great service in establishing—it was practically impossible for Vavasor Griffiths, who had an important school at Maesgwyn, to teach at Llwynllwyd ; secondly, that there is no evidence that Vavasor Griffiths was ever at Llwynllwyd ; while, again, there is bound up with this second part of the argument, the statement that it was Dr. Thomas Rees in his *History of Protestant Nonconformity*, who, out of stupidity (' hurtrwydd ') first gave rise, in 1861, to the idea of Vavasor Griffiths's connexion with Llwynllwyd.

Mr. Shankland's article has been replied to by the late Rev. D. Edmondes Owen, M.A., then Vicar of Llandovery,

in an English article on ' Who was Williams Pantycelyn's
Tutor at Llwynllwyd ? ' in *The Journal of the Calvinistic
Methodist Historical Society*, vol. iv, no. 4, September
1919. This article shows Mr. Shankland's assumption
with regard to Dr. Thomas Rees to have been entirely
false. Mr. Edmondes Owen quotes David Peter, a
historian of eminence, who, from 1789 to 1792, was tutor
at this very Academy after its return to Carmarthen, and
who, in 1816, published a great work *Hanes Crefydd yn
Nghymru* (' The History of Religion in Wales '), in the
appendix to which (p. 683) he says (the translation is ours)
' On the death of Mr. Perrot in the year 1733, Mr. Vavasor
Griffiths of Llwynllwyd, near the Hay, in Breconshire, was
chosen tutor in his place, and the academy was removed
to Llwynllwyd—[i. e. from Carmarthen] . . . He [Vavasor
Griffiths] finished his course in the year 1741.' This
quotation, given by Mr. Edmondes Owen, proves that
Dr. Thomas Rees, in 1861, was not the first to associate
Vavasor Griffiths with Llwynllwyd. Mr. Edmondes Owen
then addresses himself to the further question of David
Peter's correctness in asserting the association. He gives
the following entries for the year 1734 which he has
found in accounts paid by a Roger Jones, attorney in
Talgarth, on behalf of his brother John Jones, who was
a student at Llwynllwyd, and who hailed, like Williams
Pantycelyn, from the neighbourhood of Llandovery :

To Mr. Price, Lloynlloyd, as p acct	£5 5s. 0d.
To my master his bill	£5 0s. 0d.

which show that in addition to David Price, who was
certainly connected with the institution, there was another
master at Llwynllwyd. An entry for 1735 :

Pd Mr. Griffiths for entrance or admission money	£0 10s. 6d.

and two entries for 1736 :

Pd Mr. Price of Lloynlloyd in pt 30th April 1736   £4 10s. 6d.
Pd 7th Octr. 1736 Mr. Griffiths by the hands of
  Mr. Price of Lloynlloyd   £1 10s. 0d.

further prove that there was a ' Mr. Griffiths ' connected
with Llwynllwyd. Lastly, Mr. Edmondes Owen, to prove
that this ' Mr. Griffiths ' was Vavasor Griffiths, gives in
full a letter, never published before, which was sent by
Vavasor Griffiths in reply to a letter which this John
Jones, after he had entered Merton College, Oxford, had
sent in 1737 to his old tutor ' Mr. Griffiths ' at Llwynllwyd.

The article in *The Journal of the Calvinistic Methodist
Historical Society* thus shows conclusively that Mr. Shankland was wrong in limiting the association of Vavasor
Griffiths to Maesgwyn, and, further, that Vavasor
Griffiths was definitely associated with Llwynllwyd.
Having established this connexion, Mr. Edmondes Owen
makes a suggestion—a reasonable suggestion in view of
the great superiority of Vavasor Griffiths's academic attainments over those of David Price—that ' the management
of the School and the catering was largely in the hands of
David Price, while the actual teaching of the senior students
was left to Mr. Griffiths '.

ii. As to the second point—the existence and the
tutorship of a school at Chancefield—light is forthcoming from Howell Harris's *Diaries*. Mr. Richard
Bennett deals with the question, with especial reference
to Mr. Shankland's article, in *The Journal of the
Calvinistic Methodist Historical Society*, vol. iv, no. 2,
January 1919. Mr. Shankland having referred to the
connexion of the Academy and Vavasor Griffiths with
Chancefield, as a ' very pretty bit of imagination '

(' dychymyg tlws iawn '), Mr. Bennett gives the following extracts from Harris's *Diaries* to substantiate his
view that there was an Academy at Chancefield, and
that Vavasor Griffiths was tutor thereat :

1739.   Aug. 16.   ' I was enlightened when with Mr. Vavasur Griffies,
               Tutor of ye Welsh Academy to see ye necessity
               of studying the knowing God more.'

    ,,   Dec. 26.   ' prayed . . . for Mr. Griff—— & his Academy, that the
               Lord would fit the young ones out for service.'

1740.   Feb. 22.   ' When I told at Chancefield to Mr. Vav. Griff——
               of my Persecution, he said I had now then
               a title to some Promises more.   One of his
               students said &c.'

    ,,   Apr. 26.   ' tow^d Chancefield to see Mr. V. Griff——.——
               there ab^t circumstantial matters to pt. 12 ;
               with the young students to pt. 1.'

    ,,   June 22.   ' from hence [Bronllys—a village hardly a mile
               distant from Talgarth] full of love and comfort
               with Mr. Griff.——'

    ,,   July 12.   ' hearing bad news of the young Academicians.'

    ,,   Sep. 18.   ' tow^d home with my dear friends Mr. V. Griffiths
               and Mr. Thos. of Gwernddyfwg [a farm about
               eight miles north-west of Talgarth] . . . *postea*
               Mr. V. Griff. and I consulted together . . . talked
               ab^t the young Academicians . . . We agreed
               of the danger of recommending those to the
               Ministry that had not tasted converting Grace
               . . . as there was so much Arminianism crept in
               already among them, . . . parted pt. 2 at
               Pen-y-genghel ' [a neighbouring farm to
               Llwynllwyd].

    ,,   Oct. 15.   ' At Chancefield had more light from Dr. Bro. Vav.
               Griff. &c. . . . *postea*, saw God's love to me in
               inclining Mr. V. Griff. meltingly to say that
               what was his was mine &c.'

These extracts make it clear that there was a school at
Chancefield, that it was called the ' Academy ', and that
Vavasor Griffiths was tutor thereat.

Thus we arrive at two facts : firstly, a school or Academy was held at each of the three places, Maesgwyn, Llwynllwyd, and Chancefield ; and secondly, Vavasor Griffiths was connected with the institution at each of the three places. It is, of course, possible that the Academy was not at the three places simultaneously. Indeed, Mr. Bennett inclines to the opinion that it was removed from Maesgwyn to Chancefield, where a school existed prior to Vavasor Griffiths's connexion with it.[1] However that may be, the triple location with a common tutor seems, on the evidence of the material so far available, fairly well established.

iii. A third question, that relating directly to our text, can now be approached. At which of these three places was Richard Price educated ? Mr. Shankland, in the article mentioned above, says it was at Maesgwyn ; but he merely says so, and does not produce a single fact to seek to prove it. On the other hand, what evidence there is seems to point definitely to Chancefield. William Morgan, admittedly not a good biographer, in his brief *Memoirs* of his uncle, agrees, nevertheless, on this particular point, though he frequently differs from her in other points, with Caroline Williams, another descendant of the Morgan family, in *A Welsh Family* which, based on family papers, gives an account of the Morgan family, and many facts about the Price family. Morgan says (p. 5) that his uncle ' was moved

[1] An entry in Howell Harris's *Diary* under 1737/Feb. 21, mentions a new Schoolmaster at Chancefield. *The Journal of the Calvinistic Methodist Historical Society—A Special Supplement : The Itinerary of Howell Harris*, by the Rev. M. H. Jones.

There is every probability that the new Schoolmaster was none other than Vavasor Griffiths, into whose charge the Academy had passed four years earlier.

to the Rev. Vavasor Griffiths's academy at Talgarth in Breconshire '. Miss Williams says (p. 4) that Richard Price was ' with a tutor at Talgarth, in Breconshire ', and again (p. 4) speaks of him as spending ' one year more at Talgarth '. Until definite evidence to the contrary is forthcoming, therefore, it is reasonable to regard ' at Talgarth in Breconshire ' as a correct description of the place where Price was educated. The description points directly and obviously to Chancefield. Moreover, the association of Vavasor Griffiths with Talgarth which we find in one of these references, agrees with the association of ' Vavasur Griffies ' with Chancefield which we find in the extracts from Harris's *Diaries*. On the evidence available, therefore, we conclude that Richard Price was educated at Chancefield, and that Vavasor Griffiths was his tutor.

BIBLIOGRAPHY

NOTE

THESE Lists have been compiled by the collation of lists and references derived from a variety of sources :

- (a) the publishers' notices of works by the same author in the several published works of Price ;
- (b) Priestley's list of Price's works appended to his funeral sermon ;
- (c) notices of Price's works in the *Gentleman's Magazine* from the year 1758 to the year 1791 ;
- (d) lists, kindly supplied by the authorities of the undermentioned libraries, or made by the writer, of works by or relating to Price which are in the possession of those libraries :

The British Museum Library, London.

The Bodleian Library, Oxford.

Dr. Williams's Library, London.

The Guildhall Library, London.

Library of Congress, Washington, U.S.A.

Yale University Library, U.S.A.

Harvard University Library, U.S.A.

New York Public Library, U.S.A.

The Public Library of the City of Boston, U.S.A.

The Library of the American Academy of Arts and Sciences, Boston, U.S.A.

The Library of the American Philosophical Society, Philadelphia, U.S.A.

The Library of the Connecticut Academy of Arts and Sciences, New Haven, U.S.A.

I. WORKS BY PRICE

A Review of the Principal Questions and Difficulties in Morals, particularly those respecting the Origin of our Ideas of Virtue, its Nature, relation to the Deity, Obligation, Subject-matter, and Sanctions.   8º London.   1st ed. 1758.
2nd ed. corrected 1769.

With a Dissertation on the Being and Attributes of the Deity.
3rd ed. corrected and enlarged 1787.

Britain's happiness and the proper improvement of it ; represented in a sermon preached at Newington Green, on Nov. 29, 1759 ; being the day appointed for a general thanksgiving. 8º Lond. 1759.

[An Essay towards solving a problem in the Doctrine of Chances. By the late Rev. Mr. Bayes, F.R.S., communicated by Dr. Price, in a letter to John Canton, A.M., F.R.S.] With an introductory letter by Dr. Price, and an appendix containing an application of the foregoing rules to some particular cases, also by Dr. Price.
Philosophical Transactions. Vol. liii, p. 370.

A Demonstration of the Second Rule in the Essay towards a solution of a problem in the Doctrine of Chances [published in Philosophical Translations, Vol. liii].
Philosophical Transactions. Vol. liv, p. 296.

The Nature and Dignity of the Human Soul. A sermon preached at St. Thomas's, January the first, 1766. For the benefit of the Charity-School in Gravel Lane, Southwark.   8º Lond. 1766.

Four Dissertations. 1. On Providence. 2. On Prayer. 3. On the reasons for expecting that virtuous men shall meet after death in a state of happiness. 4. On the importance of Christianity, the nature of historical evidence, and Miracles.   8º Lond.   1st ed. 1767.
2nd ed. 1768.
3rd ed. 1772.
4th ed. 1777.

Observations on the Expectations of Lives, the increase of mankind, the influence of great towns on population, and particularly the state of London, with respect to the healthfulness and number of its inhabitants. In a Letter to Benjamin Franklin, Esq., LL.D. and F.R.S   Philosophical Transactions. Vol. lix, p. 89.

Observations on the proper method of calculating the values of reversions depending on Survivorships.

Philosophical Transactions.   Vol. lx, p. 268.

On the effect of the aberration of light on the time of a Transit of Venus over the Sun. In a Letter to Benjamin Franklin, Esq., LL.D. and F.R.S.   Philosophical Transactions.   Vol. lx, p. 536.

The vanity, misery, and infamy of knowledge without suitable practice ; represented in a sermon preached at Hackney, Nov. 4, 1770.   8° Lond. 1770.

Observations on Reversionary Payments ; on Schemes for providing Annuities for Widows and Persons in Old Age ; on the Method of calculating the values of Assurances on Lives, and on the National Debt.   To which are added four essays on different subjects in the doctrine of Life Annuities and Political Arithmetic. Also Tables showing the probabilities of life in London, Norwich, and Northampton.   8° Lond. 1771.

2nd ed. 1772.

3rd ed. much enlarged 1773.

4th ed. enlarged by additional notes and essays into two volumes 1783.

5th ed. with algebraical notes by William Morgan, 2 vols. 1792.

6th ed. with algebraical notes by William Morgan, 2 vols. 1803.

An Appeal to the Public on the Subject of the National Debt.

8° Lond. 1st—4th eds., 1772-7.

On the insalubrity of marshy situations. In a letter to the Rev. Dr. Horsley.   Philosophical Transactions.   Vol. lxiv, Pt. 1, p. 96.

Observations on the difference between the duration of Human Life in Towns and Country Parishes and Villages.

Philosophical Transactions.   Vol. lxv, Pt. 2, p. 424.

Short and easy Theorems for finding, in all cases, the differences between the values of annuities payable yearly, and of the same annuities payable half-yearly, quarterly, or monthly. In a Letter to Sir John Pringle, Bart., President of the Royal Society.

Philosophical Transactions.   Vol. lxvi, Pt. 1, p. 109.

Observations on the nature of Civil Liberty, the Principles of Government, and the Justice and Policy of the war with America ; to which are added an appendix and postscript containing a state of the national debt, an estimate of the taxes and an account of the national income and expenditure since the last war.

8ᵛᵒ Lond. 1st—13th eds. Lond. 1776.
Boston, Reprinted, 1776.
New York, Reprinted, 1776.
Philadelphia, Reprinted, 1776.
Dublin, Reprinted, 1776.
Edinburgh, Reprinted, 1776.

Additional Observations on the nature and value of Civil Liberty, and the War with America : also observations on schemes for raising money by public loans ; an historical deduction and analysis of the national debt ; and a brief account of the debts and resources of France. 8º Lond. 1st—3rd eds. Lond. 1777.
Dublin, Reprinted, 1777.
Philadelphia, Reprinted, 1778.

Two Tracts on Civil Liberty, the war with America, and the Finances of the Kingdom ; with a General Introduction and Supplement. 8º Lond. 1st—2nd eds. Lond. 1778.

The General Introduction and Supplement [separately].
8º Lond. 1778.
Philadelphia, Reprinted, 1778.

A Free Discussion of the doctrines of Materialism and Philosophical Necessity, in a correspondence between Dr. Price and Dr. Priestley. To which are added, by Dr. Priestley, an introduction, explaining the nature of the controversy, and letters to several writers . . .
8º Lond. 1778.

An Essay on the present state of Population in England and Wales. [In Doctrine of Annuities by Wm. Morgan.] 8º Lond. 1779.

A sermon, delivered to a congregation of Protestant Dissenters at Hackney, on the 10th of February last, being the day appointed for a general fast. With Postscript containing remarks on a passage in the Bishop of London's sermon on Ash-Wednesday, 1779.
8º 1st—4th eds. Lond. 1779.

Facts : addressed to the landholders, stockholders, merchants, farmers, manufacturers, tradesmen, proprietors of every description, and generally to all the subjects of Great Britain and Ireland. [In collaboration with John Horne Tooke.] 8º 1st—8th eds. Lond. 1780.

An Essay on the Population of England, from the Revolution to the present time. With an appendix, containing remarks on the account of the population, trade, and resources of the kingdom, in Mr. Eden's letters to Lord Carlisle. 8ᵛᵒ 1st—2nd eds. Lond. 1780.

A discourse addressed to a congregation at Hackney on Feb. 21st, 1781 ; being the day appointed for a public fast.

8° 1st ed. Lond. 1781.

2nd—4th eds. Lond. 1790.

2nd ed. Dublin, 1790.

The State of the Public Debts and Finances at signing the Preliminary Articles of Peace, in January, 1783. With a plan for raising money by public loans, and for redeeming the public debts.

8° 1st—2nd eds. Lond. 1783.

Postscript to this.   8° Lond. 1784.

A collection of the Letters . . . addressed to the Volunteers of Ireland, on the subject of a Parliamentary Reform ; by the Earl of Effingham, Dr. Price [and others].   8° Lond. 1783.

Observations on the Importance of the American Revolution, and the means of making it a benefit to the world.

8° and 16° 1st ed. Lond. 1784.

8° and 16° 2nd ed. Lond. 1785.

Boston, Reprinted, 1784, 1812, 1818, 1820.

Dublin, Reprinted, 1785.

Postscript to Mr. William Morgan's ' Observations on the Light of Bodies in a State of Combustion '.

Philosophical Transactions.   Vol. lxxv, Pt. 1, p. 211.

Letter introducing Dr. Clarke's ' Observations on some causes of the excess of mortality of Males above that of Females '.

Philosophical Transactions.   Vol. lxxvi, Pt. 2, p. 349.

[A Statute of Virginia. An Act for establishing religious freedom passed in the Assembly of Virginia . . . 1786.] With a prefatory letter by R. P. [i. e. Richard Price].

Single Sheet Folio, Lond. 1786.

Sermons on the Christian Doctrine as received by the different denominations of Christians. To which are added Sermons on the Security and Happiness of a Virtuous Course, on the Goodness of God and the Resurrection of Lazarus. 8° 1st—2nd eds. Lond. 1787.

Another ed. Bost. 1794, 1815.

The Evidence for a future period of Improvement in the State of Mankind, with the means and duty of promoting it, represented in a discourse delivered on Wednesday, the 25th of April, 1787, at the Meeting-house in the Old Jewry, London, to the supporters of a new Academical Institution among Protestant Dissenters. 8º Lond. 1787.

A Discourse on the Love of Our Country, delivered on Nov. 4, 1789, at the Meeting-house in the Old Jewry, to the Society for commemorating the Revolution in Great Britain. With an Appendix, containing the Report of the Committee of the Society ; an account of the population of France ; and the Declaration of Rights by the National Assembly of France. 8º 1st—2nd eds. Lond. 1789.
3rd—5th eds. Lond. 1790.
Another ed. Lond. 1790.
Dublin, 2nd ed. Reprinted, 1790.
Boston, Reprinted, 1790.
Paris, Printed in French, 1790.

Additions to Dr. Price's Discourse on the Love of Our Country, containing communications from France, occasioned by the Congratulatory Address of the Revolution Society to the National Assembly of France ; with the answers to them. 8º Lond. 1790.
Another ed. Lond. 1790.

Preface and additions to the [third edition of the] Discourse on the Love of Our Country. 8º Lond. 1790.

[This is a separate publication from the ' Additions ' and was afterwards reprinted with the 4th ed.]

Britain's Happiness and its full Possession of Civil and Religious Liberty, briefly stated and proved. 8º Lond. 1791.

Sermons by Richard Price and Joseph Priestley. 8º Lond. 1791.
Reprinted Lond. 1830.

Sermons ; In Vol. III of Unitarian Tracts. 8º Lond. 1791.
In Vol. IX of Unitarian Tracts. 8º Lond. 1836.

[Three of the Sermons (by Price) are the same in both Vols. :
I. Security of Virtuous Course.
II. Happiness of Virtuous Course.
III. Resurrection of Lazarus.]

Sermons on various subjects. 8º Lond. 1816.

N

II. WORKS OCCASIONED BY PRICE

Relating to Reversionary Payments and the National Debt.

Remarks on Dr. Price's Observations on Reversionary Payments.
Signed : Amicus.   8° Lond. 1772.

Remarks upon Dr. Price's ' Appeal to the public ' on the subject
of the national debt. Addressed to the Author.
                                        8° London : J. Wilkie, 1772.

Wimpey (J.). The Challenge ; or Patriotism put to the test,
in a letter to the Rev. Dr. Price ; occasioned by his late publications
on the National Debt.   8° Lond. 1772.

Brand, Charles. A Treatise on Assurances . . . with several
objections against Dr. Price's Observations on the Amicable Society,
&c.   8° Lond. 1775.

Laurie, J. Tables of simple and compound Interest . . . to which
are subjoined a few remarks in which Dr. Price's Observations on
Reversionary Payments . . . are proved to be erroneous.
                                                      8° Edinburgh, 1776.

Clark, Samuel. A Letter to R. Price . . . containing an entire
refutation of his treatise on Observations on Reversionary Payments,
&c.   8° Lond. 1777.

A Supplement to Calculations of the Value of Annuities ; Published for the use of Societies for benefit of Age, &c., &c. . . . To
which are added a Table and Observations to elucidate the subject
of the National Debt, occasioned by Mr. Laurie's few Remarks upon
Dr. Price's Observations. [By Mr. Dale.]   Lond. 1778.

Masères, Francis. The Principles of the doctrine of Life Annuities
. . . with a variety . . . of Tables. (Directions for using the Tables . . .
by Dr. R. Price.)   4° Lond. 1783.

Ackland, John ; Rector of Broad-Clist. A plan for rendering the
poor independent of public contribution ; founded on the basis of
the Friendly Societies, commonly called Clubs . . . To which is added,
a letter from Dr. Price, containing his sentiments and calculations
on the subject.   8° Lond. 1786.

Baily, Francis. Tables for the purchasing and renewing of leases
. . . Appendix containing . . . some remarks on the method adopted
by Dr. Price and Mr. Morgan for finding the value of annuities.
8° Lond. 1802.

Rouse, W. An investigation of the errors of all writers on
Annuities, including those of . . . Dr. Price.   8° Lond. 1816.

Benwell, J. B. An Essay on Interest and Annuities . . . with
a critical review of De Moivre's and Dr. Price's methods, &c.
8° Lond. 1821.

Relating to Civil Liberty.

[Ferguson, Adam, LL.D.] Remarks on a pamphlet lately published by Dr. Price, intitled, Observations on the nature of civil
liberty, the principles of government, and the justice and policy of
the war with America. In a letter from a gentleman in the country
to a member of Parliament.   8° Lond. 1776.

[Lind, John.] Three letters to Dr. Price ; containing remarks on
his Observations on the nature of civil liberty, the principles of
government, and the justice and policy of the war with America.
By a member of Lincoln's-Inn, F.R.S., F.S.A.   8° Lond. 1776.

Fletcher, John William. American patriotism farther confronted
with reason, scripture and the constitution : being observations on
the dangerous politics taught by the Rev. Mr. Evans . . . and the
Rev. Dr. Price. With a scriptural plea for the revolted colonies.
8° Shrewsbury, 1776.

Printed and sold at the New Chapel, and at the Rev. Mr. Wesley's
Preaching-houses, 1791.

[Goodricke, Henry.] Observations on Dr. Price's theory and
principles of civil liberty and government ; preceded by a letter to
a friend on the pretensions of the American colonies in respect of
right and equity.   8° York, 1776.

[Macpherson, James.] The rights of Great Britain asserted against
the claims of America ; being an Answer to the Declaration of the
General Congress . . . To which is now added a refutation of Dr. Price's
State of the National Debt.   8° Lond. 1776.

[Published anonymously at the instance of the British Government.]

[Authorship also attributed to Sir John Dalrymple and to Lord George Germain.]

[Shebbeare, John.]   An Essay on the origin, progress and establishment of national society ; in which the principles of government, the definitions of . . . Liberty, contained in Dr. Price's Observations . . . are . . . examined and . . . refuted.   8º Lond. 1776.

Wesley, John.   Some Observations on Liberty, occasioned by a late tract.   8º Lond. 1776.

Stewart, James.   The total refutation and political overthrow of Dr. Price, and Great Britain successfully vindicated against all American Rebels, and their advocates, &c., &c.   8º Lond. 1776.

King, William, LL.D.   An Essay on Civil Government . . . To which is added a Remonstrance with the Court of Common Council on their presenting the freedom of the city to Dr. Price for his Observations on Civil Liberty.   8º Lond. 1776.

[Moir, J.]   Obedience the best Charter ;   or law the only sanction of liberty.   In a letter to the Rev. Dr. Price.   8º Lond. 1776.

Brand, John.   Observations on . . . Mr. Gilbert's Bill ; to which are added remarks deduced from Dr. Price's account of the National Debt.   8º Lond. 1776.

Experience preferable to Theory.   An answer to Dr. Price's Observations on Civil Liberty, and the justice and policy of the war with America.   [? Gov. Thomas Hutchinson.]   8º Lond. 1776.

Bedlam, a ball, and Dr. Price's Observations on the nature of Civil Liberty.   A poetical medley.   8º Lond. 1776.

D. T.   A letter to the Rev. Dr. Richard Price on his Observations on the nature of Civil Liberty.   8º Lond. 1776.

Civil Liberty asserted, and the rights of the subject defended, against the anarchical principles of Dr. Price . . . By a Friend to the Rights of the Constitution.   8º Lond. 1776.

The Duty of the King and Subject on the principles of Civil Liberty :   Colonists not entitled to self government or to the same

privileges with Britons ; being an answer to Dr. Price's System of
Fanatical Liberty. By the author of the Political Looking-Glass.

8° Lond. 1776.

The honour of parliament and the justice of the nation vindicated ;
in reply to Dr. Price's ' Observations on the nature of civil liberty '.

8° Lond. 1776.

A Letter to the Rev. Dr. Price, wherein his Observations on the
nature of Civil Liberty . . . are candidly examined . . . also the true
principles of liberty, explained and demonstrated . . . By a Lover of
Peace and Good Government.   8° Lond. 1776.

Licentiousness unmask'd ; or Liberty explained.   [In answer to
Dr. Price's pamphlet on Civil Liberty.]   8° Lond. [1776].

Remarks on Dr. Price's Observations on the nature of civil
liberty, &c.   8° Lond. 1776.

Cursory Remarks on Dr. Price's Observations on the nature of
Civil Liberty . . . By a Merchant.   8° Lond. 1776.

Cursory Observations upon Dr. Price's Essay on Civil Liberty,
particularly relating to specie and paper currency ; by which several
of his positions are proved erroneous.   8° Lond. 1776.

Martin, John.   Familiar dialogues between Americus and Britan-
nicus ; in which the right of private judgment ; the exploded
doctrines of infallibility, passive obedience, and non-resistance ;
with the leading sentiments of Dr. Price, on the nature of civil
liberty are particularly considered.   8° Lond. 1776.

A Letter to the Rev. Dr. Price. By the author of the Defence of
the American Congress, in reply to Taxation no Tyranny.

8° Lond. 1776.

[' Taxation no Tyranny : an Answer to the Resolutions and
Address of the American Congress ' was published anonymously
in 1775—i. e. before Price's ' Civil Liberty '—and was known to
have been written by Dr. Johnson, a pensioner of the Government.]

[The ' Defence of the resolutions and address of the American
Congress in reply to Taxation no Tyranny ' is signed ' Regulus '.
The ' Monthly Review' for May 1776, vol. liv, p. 407, states that the
writer was ' probably Mr. N——e ', and Sabin (*Bibl. amer.*) enters
under ' Nourse '.]

A compleat answer to Mr. Wesley's Observations upon Dr. Price's Essay on Civil Liberty ; by a gentleman of Northumberland.

8º Newcastle, n. d.

Lord Archbishop of York, William. A Sermon preached before the Incorporated Society for the Propagation of the Gospel in Foreign Parts, Feb. 21, 1777.   Lond. 1777.

Burke, Edmund. Letters to the Sheriffs of Bristol.

8º Lond. 1777.

Gray, John. Doctor Price's notions of the nature of civil liberty shown to be contradictory to reason and Scripture.   8º Lond. 1777.

Dodd, A. Charles. The Contrast : or Strictures on select parts of Doctor Price's Additional Observations on Civil Liberty, &c.

8º Lond. 1777.

A Letter to Dr. Price on his Additional Observations on the nature and value of Civil Liberty.   8º Lond. 1777.

Wimpey, Joseph. Letters occasioned by three dialogues concerning Liberty ; . . . to which are added remarks on Dr. Price's additional observations on the nature and value of civil liberty.

Lond. 1778.

Stevenson, John. Letters in Answer to Dr. Price's two pamphlets on civil liberty.   8º Lond. 1778.

[The fifteen letters in reply to Price's ' Observations ' and the first two on the ' Additional observations ' originally appeared in the ' Public ledger ' ; the 3rd and the 14th of the 20 in the latter series were first printed in the ' Morning Chronicle '.]

Three letters to the Rev. Dr. Price : containing remarks upon his fast-sermon. By a cobbler.   8º Lond. 1779.

Pitt, G., Baron Rivers. Letters to a Young Nobleman upon . . . Government and Civil Liberty. Wherein occasion is taken to remark on the writings of . . . the Reverend Doctor Price.   8º Lond. 1784.

Relating to Materialism and Necessity.

Philalethes Rusticanus. Reflections on the Doctrines of Materialism . . . With an appendix . . . stating the substance of a correspondence between Dr. Priestley and Dr. Price on the subject.

8º Lond. 1779.

Dawes, Mathew. Philosophical Considerations, or a free enquiry into the merits of a controversy between Dr. Priestley and Dr. Price, on matter and spirit.   8° Lond. 1780.

Miscellaneous Observations on some points of the Controversy between the Materialists and their Opponents.   Lond. 1780.

A Slight Sketch of the Controversy between Dr. Priestley and his Opponents on the Subject of his Disquisitions on Matter and Spirit.
Lond. 1780.

Cooper (Thomas). A Sketch of the Controversy on Materialism.
Lond. 1789.

Butterworth, Lawrence. Thoughts on Moral Government and Agency . . . Also, strictures on Dr. Priestley's correspondence with Dr. Price on the same subject.   8° Evesham, 1792.

Relating to the Population of the Kingdom.

Four Letters to the Earl of Carlisle, from William Eden, Esq., on certain perversions of Political Reasoning . . . on the Public Debts, on the Public Credit, and the means of raising Supplies, &c.
Lond. 1780.

Howlett, Rev. John. An examination of Dr. Price's Essay on the Population of England and Wales ; and the doctrine of an increased population in this kingdom established by facts.
Maidstone : The Author [1781].

Wales, William. An Enquiry into the State of Population in England and Wales, and the proportion which the present number of inhabitants bears to the number at former periods. Lond. 1781.

[? Howlett, J.] Uncertainty of the present Population of the Kingdom, deduced from a candid review of the accounts lately given of it by Dr. Price on the one hand, and Mr. Eden, Mr. Wales, and Mr. Howlett, on the other.   8° Lond. 1781.

Chalmers, George. An estimate of the comparative strength of Britain during the present and four preceding Reigns. . . . To which is added an Essay on Population by the Lord Chief Justice Hale.
Lond. 1783.

Relating to Sermons.

Keate (Rev. William, Rector of Laveston). A free examination of Dr. Price's and Dr. Priestley's Sermons, with a Postscript containing some strictures upon an Address to the opposers of the Repeal of the Corporation and Test Acts.   8° Lond. 1790.

Relating to the Love of Our Country.

Holloway, John. A letter to Dr. Price. Containing a few strictures upon his sermon entitled, 'The love of our country'. 8° Lond. 1789.

[Bradshaw, —.] A scourge for the Dissenters, or nonconformity unmasked ; occasioned by the application intended to be made . . . for the repeal of the Corporation and Test Acts. With animadversions on Dr. Price's sermon, preached at the Old Jewry . . . 4th of November, 1789 . . . By an ecclesiastic.

Coxe, Wm. ; Archdeacon of Wilts. A Letter to . . . R. Price upon his ' Discourse on the Love of our Country ' to the society for commemorating the revolution in Great Britain.   8° Lond. 1790.

Croft, George, Vicar of Arncliffe. The Test Laws defended. A sermon . . . with . . . remarks on Dr. Price's Revolution sermon.
8° Birmingham, 1790.

Hobson, John. A series of remarks upon a sermon . . . entitled, ' The Test Laws defended ', by George Croft, D.D. . . . Prefaced by animadversions on his preface containing remarks on Dr. Price's Revolution Sermon, and other publications.   8° Birmingham, 1790.

Theodosius ; or A solemn admonition to Protestant Dissenters on the proposed Repeal of the Test and Corporation Acts ; in which are considered the political and religious characters of Dr. P . . ., Dr. Price, Mr. Fox, Judge . . ., Mr. Sheridan, Mr. B . . ., Mr. Sawbridge, Mrs. F . . ., &c.   Lond. 1790.

A Controversial Letter of a new kind to . . . Dr. Price, from a Clergyman of the Church of England. Occasioned by his Revolution sermon.   8° Lond. 1790.

Observations on Dr. Price's Revolution Sermon, and on the conduct of the Dissenters and Mr. Pitt respecting the repeal of the Test Act. [By Edward Sayer ?]   8° Lond. 1790.

Burke, Edmund. Reflections on the Revolution in France, and
on the Proceeding in certain Societies in London relative to that
Event ; in a Letter intended to have been sent to a gentleman in
Paris, 1790.   8º Lond. 1790.

Observations on the Reflections of the Right Hon. Edmund Burke
on the Revolution in France ; in a Letter to Earl Stanhope. [Sup-
posed by Mrs. Macaulay Graham.]   Lond. 1790.

Wolstencraft, Mary. A Vindication of the Rights of Men ; in
a Letter to the Right Honourable Edmund Burke, occasioned by his
Reflections on the Revolution in France.   Lond. 1791.

Priestley, Joseph, LL.D., F.R.S. Letters to the Right Honourable
Edmund Burke, occasioned by his Reflections on the Revolution in
France, &c.   8º Birmingham, 1791.

A Vindication of the Right Honourable Edmund Burke's Reflections on the Revolution in France ; in Answer to all his Opponents.
                                                       8º Lond. 1791.

Paine, Thomas. The Rights of Man ; in answer to Mr. Burke's
attack on the French Revolution.   8º Lond. 1791.

Mackintosh, James. Defence of the French Revolution and its
English Admirers against the accusation of the Right Hon. Edmund
Burke.   8º Lond. 1791.

Complete Refutation of Dr. Price, in answer to the Observations,
&c., on his Revolution Sermon, by Anti-Price.

Review of Dr. Price's Sermon on the Love of Our Country. By
A True Whig.

Dr. Price and the rights of man ! An elegy sacred to the memory
of that . . . Divine . . . and . . . Philanthropist. By H. R. H.
                                                        8º Lond. 1791.

A New Friend on an Old Subject.   8º Lond. 1791.

Wyvill, Cristopher. A defence of Dr. Price and the reformers
of England.   8º York, 1792.

Vialls, J. ; Edited by. A blow at the root ; or, Constitutional
liberty preferable to Jackobinism and anarchy (being a short
extract from a deceased author).   8º Lond. 1794.

III. WORKS ON PRICE

[Briefer notices are omitted here. Several such are, however,
referred to in the text.]

Kippis, Andrew. An address, delivered at the interment of the
late Rev. Dr. Richard Price, on the twenty-sixth of April, 1791.
8° Lond. 1791.

Priestley, Joseph. A discourse on occasion of the death of Dr.
Price ; delivered at Hackney, on Sunday, May 1, 1791.
8° Lond. 1791.

Wright, Thomas. The death of a great man improved. A sermon
in consequence of the decease of the Rev. R. Price, D.D.
8° Bristol, 1792.

Morgan, William. Memoirs of the life of the Rev. Richard
Price, D.D., F.R.S.   8° Lond. 1815.

Cromwell, Thomas. The late Richard Price, D.D., F.R.S. . . .
characterised in a sermon, preached at Newington-Green Chapel,
October 23, 1842. . . . With an introductory memoir of Dr. Price,
and the inscription on his monument.   12° Lond. 1842.

Williams, Caroline E. A Welsh Family.
Printed for private circulation, 1867.

Letters to and from Richard Price, D.D., F.R.S. 1767–90.
Reprinted from the Proceedings of the Massachusetts Historical
Society, May 1903.   Cambridge [Mass. U.S.A.] 1903.

Historical Sketches of Glamorgan, Vol. II ; Paper by Howell
Prosser.   8° Lond. and Cardiff, 1912.

Encyclopedia Britannica, 9th and 10th editions, Article on
' Richard Price ', by Professor T. Fowler.

Dictionary of National Biography, Article on ' Richard Price ',
by Professor T. Fowler.

Encyclopedia Britannica, 11th edition, Article on ' Richard Price ',
by J. M. Mitchell.

INDEX

I. PROPER NAMES

[Names occurring only in the Bibliography are omitted.]

II. GENERAL

Price, Richard, love of mankind, 140, 145, 153–4.
—, —, humility, 156–9.
—, —, manners, 158, 159.
—, —, popularity, 57, 91, 154–5.
—, —, religion, 159–69.
—, —, theological views, 10, 19, 26, 115–18.

Rational School, 33–4.
rationalism, 1.
reason, 36.
—, conquests of, 1.
—, intuitive, 35, 37.
—, practical, 35.
—, theoretical, 35.
—, = Understanding, 35.
rectitude, a law, 36–7.
—, = Virtue, 36.
Reflections on the French Revolution, 130.
Reversionary Payments, 54–63, 137.
Review of the Principal Questions in Morals, 29–37.
republic, *see* government.
resurrection of the body, 91.
right, a simple idea, 35.
— and wrong, 33, 35.
Rights of Man, 130, 133.
Revolution, American, calls forth *Civil Liberty*, 73 ff.
—,—,encouraged by Price,71–3.
—, —, ends in recognition of Independence, 96.
—, —, leads to Declaration of Independence, 78.
—,—, opinion in England about, 68–70.
—, —, opinion in Scotland about, 70–1.
—, —, Welshmen and, 82.
—, English of 1688, 1, 2, 24, 121, 128, 132.
—, —, principles of, 127.
—, —, commemoration of, *see* Society, Revolution.
—, French, cause of, 120–1.
—, —, celebration of, in Birmingham, 141.
—, —, celebration of, in London, 124–31, 134–5, 136, 140–1.

Revolution, American, opinion in England about, 122.
—, —, opinion in Germany about, 122.
— ,—, outbreak of, 121–2.

scepticism, 47.
self-determination, *see* liberty.
Sentimental School, 33–4.
Sermons on Christian Doctrine, 114–16.
Societies, Patriotic, 129, 132, 141–2, 143.
Society, Constitutional, 133, 141.
—, for promoting knowledge of Scriptures, 100–1.
—, Revolution, 123, 134, 135, 142, 145.
—, Royal, 39, 42, 42 n., 53, 147 n.
—, —, Philosophical Transactions, 42, 53.
Socinianism, 2, 66, 115–16.
soul separate from body, 90–1.
spirit, = thinking intelligent nature, 90.
—, is one, 91.

Tavern, Crown and Anchor, 134, 140.
—, London, 124, 130, 135.
taxation, American, 68.
testimony, regard due to, 46–7.
Theological College, Brecon, 4, 14.
—, Carmarthen, 4, 14, 113.
Theological Repository, 65, 101.
thought, denied to matter, 90–1.
Treaty of Paris, 96.
Trust, Daniel Williams's, 41.
truth, 126.
Two Tracts on Civil Liberty, 86.

Understanding, the, 35, 37, 46.
United States of America, constitution of, 79, 81.

virtue, 92, 110, 126, 129.
—, a law, 36–7.
—, = rectitude, 36.

war, plan to prevent, 79–81.
world, citizens of the, 126.